# Finding Self-Compassion

## A Mindfulness Workbook for Getting to Know and Love Yourself

### SYDNEY SPEARS, PhD, LSCSW

**SPRUCE BOOKS**

A Sasquatch Books Imprint

I lovingly dedicate this book to my family: Chester, Kelly, Christy, Elise, Benjamin, June, and Susan; to the developers of the Mindful Self-Compassion training program: Kristin Neff, PhD, and Christopher Germer, PhD; and to my supervisor and mentor at the Center for Mindful Self-Compassion: Steven Hickman, PsyD.

Printed in China

SPRUCE BOOKS with colophon is a registered trademark of Penguin Random House LLC

26 25 24 23 22          9 8 7 6 5 4 3 2 1

Editor: Sharyn Rosart   |   Production editor: Rachelle Longé McGhee
Designer: Alison Keefe   |   Cover design: Alicia Terry

ISBN: 978-1-63217-417-8

Spruce Books, a Sasquatch Books Imprint
1325 Fourth Avenue, Suite 1025
Seattle, WA 98101

SasquatchBooks.com

# CONTENTS

# FOREWORD

Life sucks sometimes. It can be confusing, scary, and lonely. When you're figuring out who you are, not to mention whether you even *like* who you are—there's a lot of pressure. If you think you don't fit in, or worry about how you look or what other people think of you, it can be painful. If you criticize or shame yourself for not being good enough—kicking yourself when you're down—it's even harder.

Luckily, self-compassion is a way of dealing with the pain of life that makes it less overwhelming. Imagine a warm, supportive friend who really cares about you and is always there for you, ready to help, picking you up when you are down. You do have such a friend: self-compassion. It's a superpower that you can call on 24/7. All you need to do is become aware when you're struggling, be kind in response, and remember that you're not alone. These are the three main ingredients of self-compassion: mindfulness, kindness, and common humanity.

Research shows that young people who are self-compassionate are happier: less stressed, less depressed, and less anxious. They're less likely to hate themselves because of how they look and are less vulnerable to bullying and peer pressure. The research also shows that instead of making you lazy, self-compassion increases your drive to work hard. Self-compassion is like a good coach who believes in you. When you fail at something, self-compassion helps you remember that all humans make mistakes. What's important is learning how to grow from the experience.

You may be thinking, "Aren't you supposed to be compassionate to other people instead of yourself?" The truth is, we need to turn compassion both inward and outward. The more you care for yourself, the more resources you'll have available to give to others. Your relationships will be better, because when your sense of worth comes from self-compassion, you aren't so dependent on other people's approval. This means you will be freer to be your true, authentic self.

So how do you gain this superpower? The secrets are in this amazing book. It's written by my friend and colleague Sydney Spears, an expert self-compassion teacher. She heads up the diversity initiative at the nonprofit I cofounded, the Center for Mindful Self-Compassion, and is also a college professor and therapist. She knows how to help young people learn to be self-compassionate—even when they doubt themselves. The book is beautiful and fun to read, and if you do the practices and exercises within it, you'll learn skills that will transform your life. I hope you enjoy it! I know I did.

—Kristin Neff, PhD

# INTRODUCTION

## WELCOME TO THIS JOURNAL!

**HI THERE!** I'm so glad you will be taking this adventure with yourself. Journaling gives you the opportunity to learn more about the one person you will be with every day, each second of your life, forever—you! Young adulthood is a great time to lean into a study of yourself because it is a period of major change and growth, when you start to figure out all your identities. This can also be challenging and confusing, but this journal is here to support you as you learn to cope while moving through these normal and natural shifts. Specifically, you are going to learn how to be compassionate to yourself. As you study yourself, there will be many opportunities for you to learn how to respond to challenges and discomfort with mindfulness and self-compassion. So get ready for this exciting journey that is all about creating the truth of you!

## WHAT IS SELF-COMPASSION?

The developer and key researcher behind the concept of self-compassion is psychologist Kristin Neff. Her groundbreaking 2003 research explored this idea and she went on, with Dr. Christopher Germer, to develop the Mindful Self-Compassion training program. There are three parts to this practice: mindfulness, common humanity, and self-kindness.

**Mindfulness** is about paying attention without judgment to whatever is happening in the present moment. This is the first step in experimenting with responding to your discomfort with self-compassion. It asks you to bring attention and focus to the moment, rather than letting yourself be distracted. Mindfulness teaches you to get to know yourself by paying attention to your thoughts, feelings, emotions, reactions, urges, and bodily sensations. It is a practice, which means that it is something you can do regularly, and the more you practice it, the easier it becomes and the more you will feel its benefits.

**Common humanity** is understanding that all people experience challenges and failures. It is a natural part of living (not only as a young person, but throughout life) to have times when you are struggling, or feel imperfect or like you are not successful. In other words, though it may feel lonely, know that you are never really alone in feeling mad, bad, or sad.

**Self-kindness** is the act of responding to your own discomfort with kindness rather than harshly judging or criticizing yourself. Think of it as treating yourself the same way a really good, close friend would with more understanding, caring, motivation, and protection. Getting into the habit of kindly supporting yourself does take some time and practice, but by completing the journal activities in this book you will learn how to do it.

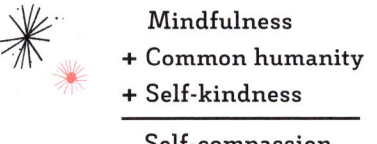

Mindfulness
+ Common humanity
+ Self-kindness
───────────────
Self-compassion

Think about treating yourself like a supergood friend in those hard moments rather than beating yourself up, overreacting, or lashing out at others. Practicing self-compassion is about bringing kindness into the process of choosing what you might need to say, think, or do in order to support yourself while you are struggling. The discomfort may still be there, but it will feel much less uncomfortable. And, as with any practice, the more you do it, the easier it gets.

## THE TENDER YOU AND THE FIERCE YOU

How do you show kindness? There is more than one approach, depending on the situation. Dr. Neff talks about how we each have a tender side and a fierce side. The tender side responds to challenging situations by comforting, soothing, and being nice. The fierce side is more about figuring out and choosing the smartest actions to take to protect yourself, advance your interests, or move out of a rut. Fierce self-compassionate actions include setting healthy boundaries, motivating yourself, and standing up for yourself.

Many teens and young adults are faced with constant pressures related to social media, school, work, parents, relationships, conflicts, careers, cultural-social identities, social injustice, and fears about the future. In this environment, it's important to be able to protect yourself and know when self-protection is needed.

# HOW CAN SELF-COMPASSION HELP ME?

The world today is restless and in flux, which can cause a lot of different worries and anxiety. In addition, young people are also figuring out their own cultural-social identities and dealing with complex social justice issues. With so much going on, it is natural to feel overwhelmed at times.

The good news is that practicing self-compassion can help you be less stressed-out and less worried by the pressures and problems facing you. Research by Dr. Neff and her colleagues shows that using self-compassion techniques can also help you to feel less depressed, withdrawn, frustrated, and self-critical. The result is that you can be far more hopeful and upbeat as you go about your life. These skills will serve you well not only right now but throughout your future.

This is why mindfulness and self-compassion are such necessary and desirable skills to have in your life. Once you have these tools in your pocket, you can help yourself any time you need self-support. This help is free and always available to you.

# WAYS TO USE THIS JOURNAL

This journal will walk you through the basics of learning self-compassion in all areas of your life, including your cultural-social identities. You will find that true self-compassion is about bringing kindness to all the parts of you.

As you read on, you will see that the book is organized into a series of eight journal adventures for you to take. Each of them offers practice in the three skills that you need for self-compassion—mindfulness, common humanity, and self-kindness. Within each journal adventure you will be invited to experiment with some interesting activities that will turn up the volume on ways that you can offer yourself acts of kindness and strong support when you need it. You will also have the chance to think about how you might be feeling before you begin each journal activity and after you've completed it.

This journal is set up so that you can write or sketch your responses in the spaces provided within each activity. (You can also use this book as a guide and write your responses in a separate journal or notebook if you need more room or if that feels better to you.) All of these activities will ask you to identify your feelings, emotions, thoughts, and bodily sensations. To help you with this, you will find a list of feelings, emotions, thoughts, and bodily sensations on pages 12–13. To discover even more of these, you can refer to the Resources section in the back of the book, which contains URLs for online sources of information.

This journal is trauma sensitive and culturally inclusive. For those of you who identify as a member of an underserved, diverse group, there are a lot of great resources throughout the book. You'll also find crisis hotline information listed in the back of the book if you need more help.

If there is ever a part of any journal activity that you would prefer to skip, please feel free to do so. You can also take breaks anytime during the activities, especially if you notice yourself feeling very emotional or if you are having a hard time focusing. Please know that you can change a particular activity to fit your body, your mind, and your world if that is more useful to you. It is actually self-compassionate to notice what you are feeling and give yourself what you might need at any time. To keep your practice going, I would suggest that you try to complete at least two to three journal activities per week, if you can.

Within each activity you will be asked to jot down any parts of the experience that you found to be really helpful to you. These helpful parts are called "keepers." You may want to keep track of your keepers—they can be especially helpful to repeat at a later time or when you might need them as self-compassionate reminders. At the end of the journal you will also be asked to jot down your top twelve keepers to use over and over.

Remember that this journal adventure is about being open to exploring and learning all about you with curiosity and fun—and not about judging yourself.

Are you ready to roll now? Happy exploring!

*Sydney Spears*

—Sydney Spears, PhD

# Feelings, Emotions, Thoughts, and Bodily Sensations

Every day we go through a range of thoughts, emotions, feelings, and bodily sensations that characterize our lived experiences. Learning to identify what you are experiencing is an essential part of mindfulness. If we cannot recognize our thoughts, emotions, feelings, and sensations, it is hard to understand ourselves or make good decisions.

It can be hard to distinguish between emotions and feelings. Some researchers define an emotion as the actual experience (for example, being rejected) and a feeling as your description of the emotion ("I feel unwanted"). A thought would be the words you use to describe your feeling ("I feel sad and bad about myself"). A bodily sensation is physical (hot or cold, for example). For the purposes of this book, we are going to list feelings and emotions together, but acknowledge that they are different from physical or bodily sensations, and also different from thoughts. When you are trying to identify what you are experiencing at any time, use the lists that follow to help you identify and name your feelings, emotions, and bodily sensations.

These word lists are adapted from the work of many different psychological and neurological researchers. They do not include every single feeling or emotion in the universe, but they should offer you a lot of different concepts and examples to help you characterize what you are experiencing. Feel free to create or add your own words to the lists.

# FEELINGS AND EMOTIONS
## POSITIVE OR NEUTRAL

| | | | | | |
|---|---|---|---|---|---|
| Accepting | Creative | Friendly | Mellow | Quiet | Special |
| Admired | Curious | Fulfilled | Merry | Reactive | Spontaneous |
| Admiring | Daring | Gentle | Mischievous | Reassured | Stimulated |
| Adventurous | Dedicated | Giving | Moved | Receptive | Stoic |
| Affectionate | Defiant | Gleeful | Natural | Reconciled | Sunny |
| Alert | Delighted | Grateful | Neutral | Reflective | Supported |
| Alive | Determined | Grounded | Nostalgic | Refreshed | Supportive |
| Amazed | Doting | Happy | Nurturing | Rejuvenated | Sympathetic |
| Amused | Dreamy | Harmonious | Nurtured | Relaxed | Strong |
| Appreciative | Eager | Healed | Obliging | Relieved | Talkative |
| Attracted | Ecstatic | Helpful | Ok | Renewed | Tender |
| Awestruck | Empathetic | Heroic | Open | Resourceful | Thankful |
| Beautiful | Empowered | Honored | Optimistic | Respected | Thoughtful |
| Blank | Enchanted | Hopeful | Outgoing | Responsible | Thrilled |
| Blessed | Encouraged | Horny | Overjoyed | Rested | Tickled |
| Blissful | Energized | Humbled | Passionate | Robust | Touched |
| Brave | Engaged | Impressed | Patient | Romantic | Tranquil |
| Bubbly | Enthusiastic | Inspired | Peaceful | Safe | Trusting |
| Buzzed | Euphoric | Interested | Perky | Satisfied | Understanding |
| Calm | Excited | Intrigued | Placid | Secure | Upbeat |
| Capable | Exhilarated | Invigorated | Playful | Self-loving | Useful |
| Caring | Expectant | Involved | Pleased | Self-reliant | Valiant |
| Centered | Exploring | Joyful | Poised | Sensible | Vibrant |
| Cheery | Fascinated | Jubilant | Powerful | Serene | Vulnerable |
| Compassionate | Fearless | Kind | Present | Settled | Warm |
| Comfortable | Festive | Likable | Professional | Sexy | Well |
| Composed | Flirtatious | Lively | Protected | Silly | Wise |
| Confident | Forgiven | Lovable | Protective | Sincere | Wonderful |
| Connected | Forgiving | Loved | Proud | Smart | Worthy |
| Content | Fortunate | Loving | Purposeful | Sociable | Zestful |
| Courageous | Free | Lucky | Questioning | Soothed | |

# NEGATIVE

| | | | | | |
|---|---|---|---|---|---|
| Abandoned | Awful | Coerced | Depleted | Distant | Exploited |
| Aggravated | Awkward | Concerned | Depressed | Distrustful | Fearful |
| Agitated | Baffled | Confused | Despairing | Disturbed | Fed up |
| Alone | Belittled | Contemptuous | Despondent | Dominant | Fidgety |
| Aloof | Betrayed | Cranky | Disappointed | Dominated | Flustered |
| Angry | Bitter | Crushed | Disconnected | Doubtful | Forlorn |
| Anguished | Blue | Cynical | Discouraged | Embarrassed | Fragile |
| Annoyed | Bored | Damaged | Disdainful | Empty | Frazzled |
| Anxious | Bullied | Defeated | Disgruntled | Enraged | Freaked out |
| Apprehensive | Burned-out | Defenseless | Disrespected | Exasperated | Frustrated |
| Ashamed | Clueless | Defiant | Dissatisfied | Exhausted | Furious |

FEELINGS AND SENSATIONS

Gloomy
Grieving
Grossed out
Grouchy
Guilty
Harassed
Hated
Heartbroken
Helpless
Hesitant
Hopeless
Hormonal
Horrified
Hostile
Humiliated
Hurt
Hypersensitive
Inadequate
Incensed
Ignored
Ill at ease
Impatient
Indecisive
Indifferent
Indignant
Inferior
Inhibited

Insecure
Insulted
Irate
Irritated
Isolated
Invisible
Jealous
Judged
Judgmental
Jumpy
Lethargic
Listless
Livid
Lonely
Longing
Mad
Mean
Melancholy
Miserable
Mistreated
Moody
Mortified
Mystified
Nasty
Nervous

Numb
Objectified
Obsessed
Offended
On edge
Oppressed
Outraged
Overworked
Overwhelmed
Panicky
Paralyzed
Paranoid
Passive
Perplexed
Persecuted
Pissed off
Pitied
Powerless
Put down
Questioned
Quarrelsome
Rattled
Rebellious

Rebuffed
Rebuked
Reckless
Regretful
Rejected
Reluctant
Remorseful
Repentant
Resentful
Resigned
Resistant
Restless
Robotic
Sad
Scared
Self-conscious
Self-critical
Selfish
Shaken
Shocked
Shut down

Silenced
Skeptical
Sorrowful
Sorry
Sour
Spiteful
Stingy
Stressed
Suspicious
Teary
Tense
Terrified
Torn
Trapped
Ugly
Uneasy
Uncomfortable
Unforgiving
Unhappy
Unsettled
Unsure

Upset
Used
Useless
Vain
Vengeful
Victimized
Vindictive
Weak
Weary
Withdrawn
Worn-out
Worried
Worthless
Yearning

# PHYSICAL OR BODILY SENSATIONS

Aching
Aroused
Bloated
Blocked
Breathless
Bruised
Burning
Butterflies in stomach
Buzzing
Chilled
Choking
Clammy
Clenched
Cold
Congested

Constricted
Cramped
Dizzy
Drained
Dry
Dull
Electric
Energetic
Faint
Floating
Fluid
Flushed
Fluttery
Frozen
Full
Goose bumps

Gurgling
Heart pounding
Heaviness
Hollowed out
Hungry
Hurting
Hot
Icy
In pain
Itchy
Knotted
Light
Limp
Loose
Lump in throat

Nauseated
Out of body
Paralyzed
Pressure
Prickly
Pulsing
Quaking
Queasy
Radiating
Rigid
Salivating
Shaky
Shivery
Sleepy
Slow
Sore

Spacey
Stiff
Still
Suffocated
Supported
Sweaty
Throbbing
Tickly
Tight
Tingling
Trembly
Twitchy
Vibrating
Wet
Wobbly
Wooden

## MY SAFER/BRAVER ACTIONS

These are my tools for calming and comforting myself. As I'm working through the adventures, if I start to feel any discomfort, I can try any of these actions to pause, calm myself, and feel more grounded. I can come back to this page at any point to remind myself of these actions and add any others that work well for me.

- [ ] Taking deep breaths, inhaling on a count of 4 and exhaling on a slow count of 6 to 8
- [ ] Pressing my feet firmly into the surface beneath me several times to ground myself
- [ ] Shifting my attention to something pleasant wherever I am right now
- [ ] Rubbing my hands together to feel some warmth
- [ ] Walking, moving, or stretching my body
- [ ] Talking to someone I can lean on for support when I need it
- [ ] Texting or calling a crisis hotline for support when really struggling a lot (USA: 988 or 1-800-273-8255)
- [ ] If I am in immediate crisis, calling 911
- [ ] .......................................................................................................
- [ ] .......................................................................................................
- [ ] .......................................................................................................

## CRISIS HOTLINE NUMBERS

If your local crisis hotline is not listed here, look up and write down your local number below, so you can easily find it (see the Resources section on page 174 for additional numbers and websites).

**USA:** 988 or 1-800-273-8255

**Canada:** 1-833-456-4566, or text 45645

**My local crisis hotline:** ...........................................................................

**Other emergency numbers:** .........................................................................

## ACTIVITIES

**Pressing My Stop-and-Notice Button**

**Checking Out the Space and Place I'm In**

## ADVENTURE #1:

## Slowing Down and Paying Attention to What I'm Doing Right Now

# PRESSING MY STOP-AND-NOTICE BUTTON

## CHECKING IN WITH MYSELF BEFORE EXPLORING TODAY'S ACTIVITY

**Circle the number below that describes how you are feeling right now.**

| 5=feeling really good now | 4=feeling good now | 3=feeling ok now | 2=not feeling good now | 1=really struggling now |

Think about all the different buttons you press every day, whether it's a microwave oven, a remote, or your smartphone. The act of pressing one of those buttons draws your attention to the present moment so that you notice what you are doing and press the button you want. Just as with buttons, you often have to slow down in life and focus in order to notice what's really going on. Otherwise, you can easily miss important information that you need in order to understand what is happening and, ultimately, to make good choices and decisions for yourself.

Imagine your mind and body as a kind of human machine that has its own pause or "stop-and-notice" button. Pressing it gives you a moment to pause your thoughts and activities and notice where you're at emotionally, physically, and mentally. Being able to press your own pause button is a useful tool—it puts you "in the moment," which is the beginning of mindfulness.

## MY STOP-AND-NOTICE BUTTON

This activity is about designing an imaginary button you can "push" to remind yourself to take a pause—a moment to stop and simply notice yourself—to see how you are feeling. Using the space on the following pages, design your personal stop-and-notice button.

- Use letters, words, body movements, sketches, images, music, or any creative content of your choice for your stop-and-notice button.
- Think about what design elements will best help you pause, notice, and focus on whatever might be happening in your space—perhaps there is a color you find calming or a snippet of music that makes you feel relaxed.

- Once you have completed designing your stop-and-notice button, test it out by "pressing" your button. Stop and notice for one to two minutes within your own orbit right now. It might be just taking a moment to really notice the space you are in or maybe to review how your body feels.

- Snap a photo of your stop-and-notice button or copy your sketch onto a piece of paper, and keep it handy. Remember that there is no limit to using your stop-and-notice button. You can use it to pause any time.

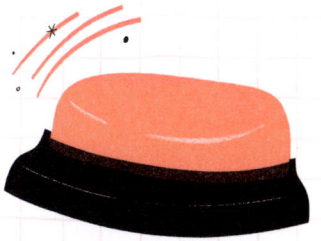

# REFLECTION ZONE

○ Jot down what you observed and noticed about yourself during today's activity. ..................................................................................

○ What thoughts came up for you during this activity?

...................................................................................................................

○ How did your body feel during this activity? (For examples, you can refer to the list on page 13.)...............................................................

...................................................................................................................

○ What feelings and emotions did you notice during this activity? (For examples, you can refer to the lists on pages 12–13.)

...................................................................................................................

○ What did you learn about yourself that really stood out to you?

...................................................................................................................

○ "Keepers" are certain parts of the journal activities that feel especially helpful to you. Did you find any parts of today's activity that you would like to keep as go-tos when you want to pause and be in the moment? If so, jot down your keepers here:..............................................................

...................................................................................................................

○ Jot down a word that can remind you to press your stop-and-notice button when needed....................................................................................

## CHECKING IN WITH MYSELF AFTER EXPLORING TODAY'S ACTIVITY

**Circle the number below that describes how you are feeling right now.**

| ☺ | ☺ | 😐 | ☹ | ☹ |
|---|---|---|---|---|
| 5=feeling really good now | 4=feeling good now | 3=feeling ok now | 2=not feeling good now | 1=really struggling now |

You explored this activity
and yourself—so cool!

# CHECKING OUT THE SPACE AND PLACE I'M IN

## CHECKING IN WITH MYSELF BEFORE EXPLORING TODAY'S ACTIVITY

**Circle the number below that describes how you are feeling right now.**

5=feeling really
good now

4=feeling
good now

3=feeling
ok now

2=not feeling
good now

1=really
struggling now

Did you know that many people, and especially younger people, often find it hard to pay attention and focus? There are so many stimuli, changes, and challenges going on all the time, from minor distractions such as social media to major issues such as social injustice, not to mention school assignments, work tasks, interactions with family and friends, bodily sensations, and so much more. All of this can make it very difficult to focus on just one thing for any period of time. It requires practice filtering out the distractions so you can learn to pay full attention to what is happening right now, in the moment.

## WHERE I AM RIGHT NOW

This activity is a simple solo attention game that can support your ability to filter out distractions and improve your focus. Practice it as often as you wish. If you have visual limitations, you can imagine your environment in your mind.

- Make sure you have a pen, pencil, or marker on hand.
- Begin this practice by pressing your stop-and-notice button. Close your eyes or drop your gaze downward for about thirty to sixty seconds to center yourself.
- Open your eyes and look around the space that you are in. Notice 10 small things—these can be things you see, smell, or feel. Try to notice these things as if it is the first time you have ever encountered them.
- Now, close your eyes or lower your gaze, and visualize the 10 things you focused on.

○ Lastly, open your eyes and list or sketch 10 small things you noticed—without looking around. This is not a test, but a simple activity for stopping and noticing—a way to practice focusing your attention and improving your ability to focus that is also fun.

# REFLECTION ZONE

- Jot down what you observed and noticed about yourself during today's activity.........................................................................................................

- What thoughts came up for you during this activity?

  .........................................................................................................................

- How did your body feel during this activity? (For examples, you can refer to the list on page 13.) ........................................................................

  .........................................................................................................................

- What feelings and emotions did you notice during this activity? (For examples, you can refer to the lists on pages 12–13.)

  .........................................................................................................................

- What did you learn about yourself that really stood out to you?

  .........................................................................................................................

- "Keepers" are certain parts of the journal activities that feel especially helpful to you. Did you find any parts of today's activity that you would like to keep as go-tos when you want to pause and be in the moment? If so, jot down your keepers here: .................................................................

  .........................................................................................................................

- Jot down a word that can remind you to notice your space and place.

  .........................................................................................................................

## CHECKING IN WITH MYSELF AFTER EXPLORING TODAY'S ACTIVITY

**Circle the number below that describes how you are feeling right now.**

| 5=feeling really good now | 4=feeling good now | 3=feeling ok now | 2=not feeling good now | 1=really struggling now |

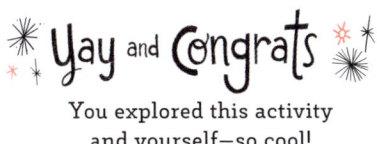

You explored this activity
and yourself—so cool!

## ACTIVITIES

**Tracking My Thoughts:
Mild, Wild, and Neutral**

**My Mixed Bag of Mind-Truths
and Mind-Untruths**

**Tracking My Rollercoaster of
Feelings and Emotions**

**Parking My Thoughts and Feelings
in the "No-Judgment Zone"**

**Responding Instead of Reacting**

**Not Today, Sneaky Inner Critic!**

# ADVENTURE #2:

## Tracking My Thoughts, Feelings, Reactions, and Responses

# TRACKING MY THOUGHTS: MILD, WILD, AND NEUTRAL

## CHECKING IN WITH MYSELF BEFORE EXPLORING TODAY'S ACTIVITY

**Circle the number below that describes how you are feeling right now.**

| | | | | |
|---|---|---|---|---|
| 5=feeling really good now | 4=feeling good now | 3=feeling ok now | 2=not feeling good now | 1=really struggling now |

Have you ever considered how many thoughts run through your mind in one day? A whole lot of them! Your mind is always cranking out stuff—real-time observations, half-remembered song lyrics, sudden realizations, random memories. A lot of this stuff is just noise, but some of these thoughts are accurate or insightful, while some others may be inaccurate, negative, or even harmful. How can you avoid being over-whelmed by it all? How can you decide what thoughts are more accurate or helpful than others? To do this, you will need to learn to curate your own mind.

One way to get started identifying the types of thoughts you're having is to label them mild, wild, or just neutral. A mild thought would be a pleasant one, such as "That breeze feels good." A neutral thought would be neither pleasant nor unpleasant, such as "It's breezy today." A wild thought would be one of the senseless, unpleasant, or harmful types, such as "I forgot my jacket, I'm such an idiot." Do not feel a need to judge these thoughts, just notice their nature, knowing that thoughts are fluid and may even shift from one category to another. This is a chance to practice noticing.

## TRACKING MY THOUGHTS

This activity is an experiment in tracking all your thoughts over a short period of time—just five minutes—to gain some understanding of whether they are mild, wild, or neutral.

- Find a comfortable place to sit or lie down.
- Press your stop-and-notice button.
- Close your eyes or drop your gaze.
- Feel your body making contact with the surface that is supporting you.

- Inhale and exhale slowly for 10 deep breaths, feeling or following each breath in and out.

- Begin to notice the thoughts that come up and categorize them as mild, wild, or neutral.

- Record each thought that comes up for the next five minutes and place a checkmark in the following chart under the appropriate category of mild, wild, or neutral.

- When five minutes are up, review your checkmarks to see how many of each type of thought you experienced; did your thoughts trend in a positive or a negative direction?

| MILD | NEUTRAL | WILD |
|---|---|---|
|  |  |  |
|  |  |  |
|  |  |  |
|  |  |  |
|  |  |  |
|  |  |  |
|  |  |  |
|  |  |  |
|  |  |  |
|  |  |  |
|  |  |  |

| MILD | NEUTRAL | WILD |
|---|---|---|
| | | |
| | | |
| | | |
| | | |
| | | |
| | | |
| | | |
| | | |
| | | |
| | | |
| | | |
| | | |
| | | |
| | | |
| **TOTAL** | **TOTAL** | **TOTAL** |
| | | |

# REFLECTION ZONE

- Jot down what you observed and noticed about yourself during today's activity.................................................................................................................

- What thoughts came up for you during this activity?

  ..........................................................................................................................

- How did your body feel during this activity? (For examples, you can refer to the list on page 13.) ....................................................................................

  ..........................................................................................................................

- What feelings and emotions did you notice during this activity? (For examples, you can refer to the lists on pages 12-13.)

  ..........................................................................................................................

- What did you learn about yourself that really stood out to you?

  ..........................................................................................................................

- Did you find any parts of today's activity that you would like to keep as go-tos when your thoughts are all over the place? If so, jot down your keepers here:...........................................................................................

  ..........................................................................................................................

- Jot down a word that can remind you to curate your thoughts.

  ..........................................................................................................................

## CHECKING IN WITH MYSELF AFTER EXPLORING TODAY'S ACTIVITY

**Circle the number below that describes how you are feeling right now.**

5=feeling really good now    4=feeling good now    3=feeling ok now    2=not feeling good now    1=really struggling now

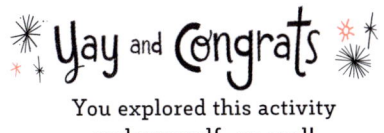

**Yay and Congrats**
You explored this activity and yourself—so cool!

# MY MIXED BAG OF MIND-TRUTHS AND MIND-UNTRUTHS

## CHECKING IN WITH MYSELF BEFORE EXPLORING TODAY'S ACTIVITY

**Circle the number below that describes how you are feeling right now.**

5=feeling really good now    4=feeling good now    3=feeling ok now    2=not feeling good now    1=really struggling now

Guess what? Just because you think something, it doesn't make it true. Young people in particular tend to believe that just because a thought comes up in their minds (especially a "wild" or negative thought) it must be totally true. The reality is that some of your thoughts are true and some are not true. So, you have to be careful about automatically believing many of the negative thoughts that arise about yourself, others, and the world. Remember that many of the negative thoughts you have tend to come from your fast brain. Your slow brain can help you reflect upon whether your negative thoughts are accurate, rather than immediately putting full faith into them. Stopping and noticing your negative thoughts can stimulate your slow brain—then you can gently and kindly question your own negative thinking.

## NOT ALL THOUGHTS ARE TRUE

This activity will be an adventure into gently questioning a particular negative thought toward yourself, someone else, or the world.

- Find a comfortable place to sit or lie down.
- Press your stop-and-notice button.
- Close your eyes or drop your gaze.
- Feel your body making contact with the surface that is supporting you.
- Inhale and exhale slowly for 10 deep breaths, feeling or following each breath in and out.
- Call to your mind a recent negative thought about yourself that you think is true and write it down.

● Now jot down the answers to the following questions:

How do you know if this thought is really true?

Is this negative thought true all the time?

What might those who love you say about your negative thought?

Even if your negative thought is partially or fully true, does it help to focus on the thought?

Do you totally believe this negative thought?

How might you bring some kindness to yourself when this negative thought arises?

What would you say to a good friend who had the same thought?

# REFLECTION ZONE

- Jot down what you observed and noticed about yourself during today's activity.........................................................................................
- What thoughts came up for you during this activity?

  ....................................................................................................
- How did your body feel during this activity? (For examples, you can refer to the list on page 13.).....................................................................
- What feelings and emotions did you notice during this activity? (For examples, you can refer to the lists on pages 12–13.)

  ....................................................................................................
- What did you learn about yourself that really stood out to you?

  ....................................................................................................
- Did you find any parts of today's activity that you would like to keep as go-tos when you need to question your negative thinking? If so, jot down your keepers here:.....................................................................

  ....................................................................................................
- Jot down a word to carry with you to keep you from automatically believing your negative thoughts..................................................................

## CHECKING IN WITH MYSELF AFTER EXPLORING TODAY'S ACTIVITY

**Circle the number below that describes how you are feeling right now.**

| 5=feeling really good now | 4=feeling good now | 3=feeling ok now | 2=not feeling good now | 1=really struggling now |

You explored this activity
and yourself—so cool!

# TRACKING MY ROLLERCOASTER OF FEELINGS AND EMOTIONS

Emotions are not all in your mind—you can also feel them in your body. If you want to know how you are truly doing at any moment, check in with how your body is reacting. For example, you might be waiting for a test to begin, and outwardly seeming very calm—but you notice that your palms are clammy. Your mind may be telling you something that you want to believe, but your body never lies! Emotions such as fear, anger, shame, disgust, happiness, sadness, surprise, and contempt are brain-body experiences. It is important to be able to identify and understand what feelings and emotions you are experiencing in order to know yourself and what you may need.

## RIDING THE FEELINGS ROLLERCOASTER

Today's activity is an invitation to name and track your emotions and feelings right now. Recognizing your feelings is the first step to learning how to speak your truth.

- Find a safe and comfortable place, indoors or outdoors.
- Press your stop-and-notice button.
- Close your eyes or drop your gaze.
- Feel your body making contact with the surface that is supporting you.
- Inhale and exhale slowly for 10 deep breaths, feeling or following each breath in and out.
- Feel free to let your muscles soften to relax as much as you can.
- Stop and notice what emotion(s) you are feeling right now.

- Jot down all the emotions you are feeling. (If you cannot find the words, check the lists of emotions and feelings on pages 12–13.)
- Repeat this activity before bedtime or tomorrow morning; notice if your feelings and emotions are the same or different during the two time periods.

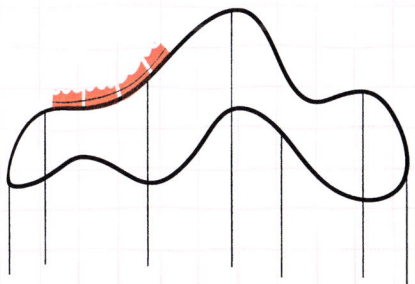

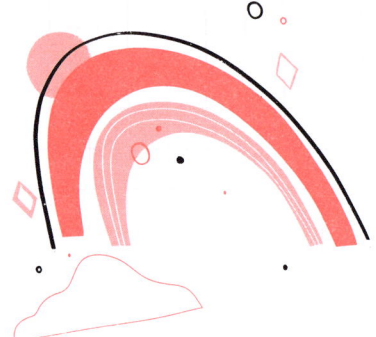

# REFLECTION ZONE

- Jot down what you observed and noticed about yourself during today's activity.................................................................................

- What thoughts came up for you during this activity?.............................
.................................................................................

- How did your body feel during this activity? (For examples, you can refer to the list on page 13.)...........................................................
.................................................................................

- What feelings and emotions did you notice during this activity? (For examples, you can refer to the lists on pages 12-13.)
.................................................................................

- What did you learn about yourself that really stood out to you?
.................................................................................

- Did you find any parts of today's activity that you would like to keep as go-tos when you need to figure out what you are feeling? If so, jot down your keepers here:......................................................................
.................................................................................

- Jot down a word or phrase that can remind you to check in with your body................................................................................

## CHECKING IN WITH MYSELF AFTER EXPLORING TODAY'S ACTIVITY

**Circle the number below that describes how you are feeling right now.**

| 5=feeling really good now | 4=feeling good now | 3=feeling ok now | 2=not feeling good now | 1=really struggling now |

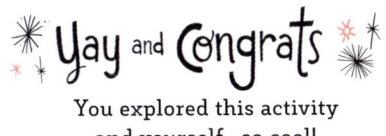

You explored this activity
and yourself—so cool!

# PARKING MY THOUGHTS AND FEELINGS IN THE "NO-JUDGMENT ZONE"

## CHECKING IN WITH MYSELF BEFORE EXPLORING TODAY'S ACTIVITY

**Circle the number below that describes how you are feeling right now.**

| 5=feeling really good now | 4=feeling good now | 3=feeling ok now | 2=not feeling good now | 1=really struggling now |

As a young person you don't have to go too far to find someone who may be judging you, especially when you are on social media. Most young people also find it all too easy to judge themselves. Critical words can exert a lot of power, and unfortunately, our body-brain tends to interpret powerful reactions as a sign of danger. It can be all too easy to quickly identify with and totally own any type of negative judgment, but try to remember that not everything that comes to your mind or the minds of others is accurate or true. Often, it is just the mind taking a walk on its wild side, which is when it tends to throw off negative, fast-brain, untrue stuff.

One thing that can help break the cycle of negativity is to stop and notice. Observe your thoughts, feelings, and emotions from a distance. Just watch your wild mind without joining the negativity. You do have a choice! The idea is to reject all judgment. Instead, observe the experience and your reactions.

## NO-JUDGMENT CALL

Today's activity is an invitation to create some space between you and your self-judgments and judgments from others so that you can stop, notice (use your slow brain), and question how much truth or untruth is really there.

- Find a comfortable place to sit or lie down.
- Press your stop-and-notice button.
- Close your eyes or drop your gaze.

- Feel your body making contact with the surface that is supporting you.
- Inhale and exhale slowly for 10 deep breaths, feeling or following each breath in and out.
- Call to mind any current thoughts, feelings, and emotions and jot down each one.
- Now imagine that you are driving a car while thinking about what you just wrote down; visualize a parking space with a sign that says "No-Judgment Zone" and pull into that space. Now see if you can test out noticing your current thoughts, feelings, and emotions without judging—just observing your experiences—no right and no wrong.

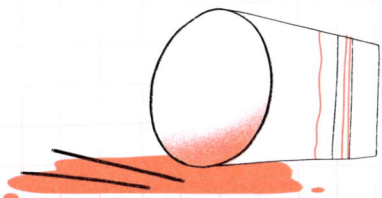

# REFLECTION ZONE

- Jot down what you observed and noticed about yourself during today's activity........................................................................................................

- What thoughts came up for you during this activity?...........................

  ...........................................................................................................

- How did your body feel during this activity? (For examples, you can refer to the list on page 13.) ........................................................................

  ...........................................................................................................

- What feelings and emotions did you notice during this activity? (For examples, you can refer to the lists on pages 12–13.)

  ...........................................................................................................

- What did you learn about yourself that really stood out to you?

  ...........................................................................................................

- Did you find any parts of today's activity that you would like to keep as go-tos when you need to turn off the urge to judge? If so, jot down your keepers here:....................................................................................................

  ...........................................................................................................

- Jot down a word or phrase that can remind you to not pass judgment on your thoughts, feelings, and emotions. .............................................................

  ...........................................................................................................

## CHECKING IN WITH MYSELF AFTER EXPLORING TODAY'S ACTIVITY

**Circle the number below that describes how you are feeling right now.**

| 5=feeling really good now | 4=feeling good now | 3=feeling ok now | 2=not feeling good now | 1=really struggling now |

You explored this activity
and yourself—so cool!

# RESPONDING INSTEAD OF REACTING

## CHECKING IN WITH MYSELF BEFORE EXPLORING TODAY'S ACTIVITY

**Circle the number below that describes how you are feeling right now.**

5=feeling really good now    4=feeling good now    3=feeling ok now    2=not feeling good now    1=really struggling now

Did you know that your brain operates at different speeds? There's your fast brain, which reacts swiftly to certain situations (such as when driving a car) and your slow brain, which responds more thoughtfully (as when considering a big question, such as "should I quit my job?"). Your fast brain tends to take over when situations are intense, threatening, or upsetting. Since life always presents us with unexpected challenges and struggles—stressors—your fast brain often jumps in with a reaction that is not always in your best interest. But you have learned that even when situations seem truly terrible, things always change and hard times do come to an end. Which means you don't want to get in the habit of letting your fast brain dictate your actions. **Reacting** is a fast-brain behavior that causes us to act out of pain and anger, and rarely improves the outcome. **Responding** is slowing down, noticing, not judging, and then thoughtfully deciding the right thing to do—and the outcomes are typically much better. Even knowing that, it is often a challenge to keep cool in the face of an unpleasant or hurtful experience.

## TRACKING MY REACTIONS

How much do you really know about how you tend to react or behave when bad stuff happens? Do you act in ways that are not the best for you or others? Today's activity will give you a window into this aspect of yourself.

- Find a comfortable place to sit or lie down.

- Press your stop-and-notice button.

- Close your eyes or drop your gaze.

- Feel your body making contact with the surface that is supporting you.

- Inhale and exhale slowly for 10 deep breaths, feeling or following each breath in and out.

- Think about the last time you reacted in a negative way to something that was a minor or medium stressor. Write or draw what happened. Then answer the following questions:

  What pushed your buttons and how did you react?

  How long did your reaction last? Did it last forever?

  What did you really need in that moment?

  How might you give yourself what you need to respond rather than just immediately reacting?

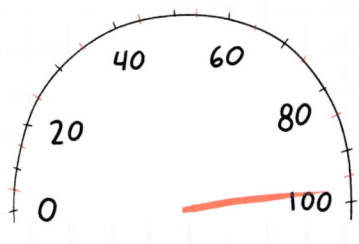

# REFLECTION ZONE

- Jot down what you observed and noticed about yourself during today's activity. ................................................................................................................

- What thoughts came up for you during this activity? ............................

..........................................................................................................................

- How did your body feel during this activity? (For examples, you can refer to the list on page 13.) ..........................................................................

..........................................................................................................................

- What feelings and emotions did you notice during this activity? (For examples, you can refer to the lists on pages 12–13.)

..........................................................................................................................

- What did you learn about yourself that really stood out to you?

..........................................................................................................................

- Did you find any parts of today's activity that you would like to keep as go-tos when you need to engage your slow brain? If so, jot down your keepers here: ......................................................................................................

..........................................................................................................................

- Jot down a word that can remind you to respond instead of reacting.

..........................................................................................................................

## CHECKING IN WITH MYSELF AFTER EXPLORING TODAY'S ACTIVITY

**Circle the number below that describes how you are feeling right now.**

5=feeling really good now    4=feeling good now    3=feeling ok now    2=not feeling good now    1=really struggling now

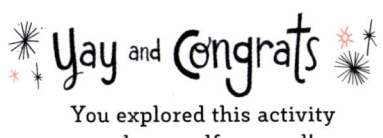

You explored this activity
and yourself—so cool!

# NOT TODAY, SNEAKY INNER CRITIC!

Guess what? Everybody has an inner critic, a voice that rises up from time to time to undermine your confidence. Something to know—inner critics are very, very sneaky. They may be quiet for a while but when you make a mistake, someone disses you, or you are just having a crappy day, guess who shows up? The dreaded inner critic likes to sneak in and make a home in your mind—where its goal is to hang out, oh, maybe forever, throwing shade about how bad you are. Don't let that happen! Give this mean control freak a chill pill.

## QUIETING MY INNER CRITIC

Today's activity is about using your fierce tenderness to stand up to your inner critic and diminish its power over you.

- Find a comfortable place to sit or lie down.

- Press your stop-and-notice button.

- Close your eyes or drop your gaze.

- Feel your body making contact with the surface that is supporting you.

- Inhale and exhale slowly for 10 deep breaths, feeling or following each breath in and out.

- Think of a recent time when you beat yourself up about something.

- Write down or draw a picture that describes what your sneaky inner critic said about you. How did you feel when that happened?

- Give your inner critic a name. Address the inner critic by name and write down what a caring friend would say to your inner critic's words about you.

- What tone of voice would your friend use?

- Out loud, read your caring friend's words to your inner critic and say those same words to yourself 10 times total (even if you don't believe the words yet). No worries if it feels weird—it takes practice to get this right.

- Notice how you feel right now and take a breath.

# REFLECTION ZONE

- Jot down what you observed and noticed about yourself during today's activity.....................................................................................

- What thoughts came up for you during this activity?.............................
  ............................................................................................................

- How did your body feel during this activity? (For examples, you can refer to the list on page 13.).........................................................
  ............................................................................................................

- What feelings and emotions did you notice during this activity? (For examples, you can refer to the lists on pages 12–13.)
  ............................................................................................................

- What did you learn about yourself that really stood out to you?
  ............................................................................................................

- Did you find any parts of today's activity that you would like to keep as go-tos when you need to vanquish your inner critic? If so, jot down your keepers here:..........................................................................................
  ............................................................................................................

- Jot down a word that can remind you that your inner critic's comments are not accurate.....................................................................................

## CHECKING IN WITH MYSELF AFTER EXPLORING TODAY'S ACTIVITY

**Circle the number below that describes how you are feeling right now.**

| 5=feeling really good now | 4=feeling good now | 3=feeling ok now | 2=not feeling good now | 1=really struggling now |

You explored this activity
and yourself—so cool!

## ACTIVITIES

My Body Talk

My Beautiful Body

My Marvelous Skin

# ADVENTURE #3:
## Tracking My Body Talk and Body Style

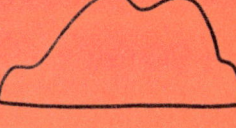

# MY BODY TALK

Do you realize that your body talks to you every day? It talks to you through the language of sensation, posture, facial expression, and gesture. Of course, it is much easier to hear what your body is saying when it sends a strong message, such as a feeling of pain. However, if you are attuned to it, you will notice that your body also regularly experiences many other types of sensations, ranging from mild to intense. These may include such feelings as tightness in your muscles, tingling in your limbs, rapid breathing, butterflies in your stomach, and temperature changes such as feeling cold or hot. These sensations provide important information about how you are really doing day-to-day. Learning to notice them is part of mindfulness. Similarly, your posture (are you hunched or standing tall?), your gestures (are you energetically moving your hands when you talk?), and your facial expressions (are you smiling? frowning?) also tell you a lot about what is going on with you in the moment. When you pay mindful attention to your body, you will be able to assess your current moods and feelings more accurately. Remember, your body does not lie!

## LISTENING TO MY BODY

This adventure is an experiment in learning to "read" your bodily sensations and expressions.

- Find a comfortable place to sit or lie down.
- Press your stop-and-notice button.
- Close your eyes or drop your gaze.
- Feel your body making contact with the surface that is supporting you.

- Inhale and exhale slowly for 10 deep breaths, feeling or following each breath in and out.

- Now scan your body and begin to notice how you are feeling. Are there any sensations that may be "talking" to you, such as tightness of certain muscles, aches, tingling, heaviness, lightness, coolness, warmth?

- Write down all the sensations that you notice.

- Now read through each one, and think about what your body talk may have been trying to tell you. For example, tightness around your jaw might be trying to let you know that you are feeling stress, frustration, or anger. On the other hand, perhaps you noticed a slight smile, meaning that you are feeling relaxed or positive.

- Next to each feeling you noted, write down what you think it might be telling you.

# REFLECTION ZONE

- Jot down what you observed and noticed about yourself during today's activity. ..............................................................................

- What thoughts came up for you during this activity? ...........................
...................................................................................................

- How did your body feel during this activity? (For examples, you can refer to the list on page 13.) ...........................................................
...................................................................................................

- What feelings and emotions did you notice during this activity? (For examples, you can refer to the lists on pages 12–13.)
...................................................................................................

- What did you learn about yourself that really stood out to you?
...................................................................................................

- Did you find any parts of today's activity that you would like to keep as go-tos when you are listening to your body? If so, jot down your keepers here: ..............................................................................
...................................................................................................

- Jot down your body-talk word that reminds you to be aware of your body's messages. .............................................................................

## CHECKING IN WITH MYSELF AFTER EXPLORING TODAY'S ACTIVITY

**Circle the number below that describes how you are feeling right now.**

| 5=feeling really good now | 4=feeling good now | 3=feeling ok now | 2=not feeling good now | 1=really struggling now |

You explored this activity
and yourself—so cool!

# MY BEAUTIFUL BODY

No two bodies are exactly the same and no body is perfect, no matter how it may look on the outside (or in a social media post!). Our bodies come in different sizes, shapes, colors, heights, abilities, and weights, with unique features and expressions. Despite this wealth of interesting differences, commercial interests and social media have promoted false ideas about what the preferred and ideal body should look like. In putting forward this notion, many—most—types of bodies are left out and, worse, are often viewed as unacceptable. With media promoting these images everywhere, it is very easy to start believing these ideas and judging your own body and even other people's bodies. Harshly criticizing your own body tends to make you feel really bad about yourself, which creates a sense of shame. Now is the time to end this painful cycle by creating a new body story that is designed by you!

## MY BODY STORY

This activity harnesses your power to create a new body-valuing story with the goal of accepting and loving your own uniquely beautiful body. Eliminating body-hating as a source of shame will lift you up and help you to stop judging others' bodies too.

- Press your stop-and-notice button.
- Sit somewhere comfortable—really comfortable.
- Inhale and exhale slowly for 10 deep breaths, feeling or following each breath in and out.
- If there is any place on your body that may need some tender loving care, place a hand gently on that area and send it some love.

- Write and/or draw a body story of positivity and kindness. Start by describing or drawing your body.

- Write about at least three parts of your body that you really value—inside and out.

- Next, write or draw something you find valuable or awe-inspiring about all the different bodies in the world.

# REFLECTION ZONE

- Jot down what you observed and noticed about yourself during today's activity. ..................................................................................................

- What thoughts came up for you during this activity? ...........................
..................................................................................................

- How did your body feel during this activity? (For examples, you can refer to the list on page 13.) ...........................................................
..................................................................................................

- What feelings and emotions did you notice during this activity? (For examples, you can refer to the lists on pages 12-13.)
..................................................................................................

- What did you learn about yourself that really stood out to you?
..................................................................................................

- Did you find any parts of today's activity that you would like to keep as go-tos when you start to mentally beat up on your body? If so, jot down your keepers here:.....................................................................
..................................................................................................

- Jot down your word to carry with you that helps you value your body.
..................................................................................................

## CHECKING IN WITH MYSELF AFTER EXPLORING TODAY'S ACTIVITY

**Circle the number below that describes how you are feeling right now.**

| 5=feeling really good now | 4=feeling good now | 3=feeling ok now | 2=not feeling good now | 1=really struggling now |

You explored this activity
and yourself—so cool!

# MY MARVELOUS SKIN

Did you know that your skin is the largest organ of your entire body—and one of the most important? More than just a big body covering, your skin is a marvel— a highly active and protective system that is working all the time to keep you healthy. We tend to focus on how our skin looks and forget all the impressive tasks it accomplishes every day, including keeping harmful agents out and holding essentials in, regulating our temperature, producing vitamins and, of course, providing sensation! So instead of focusing on the color, age, texture, imperfections, bumps, or markings you have on your skin, think about how amazing it is. Many young people don't like certain aspects of their skin and complain, judge, or even damage their own skin. It is time to bring some kindness specifically to your skin. Shaming yourself makes you feel worse. You have choices about your thoughts, so why not choose to love the skin you're in?

## THE SKIN I'M IN

This activity is about bringing some love and kindness to your amazing skin.

- Press your stop-and-notice button.
- Sit somewhere comfortable—really comfortable.
- Inhale and exhale slowly for 10 deep breaths, feeling or following each breath in and out.
- If there is any place on your body that may need some tender loving care, place a hand gently on that area and send it some love.

- Now begin to mindfully stop and notice the skin on your hands, arms, and/ or feet. Look at some of the details of your skin that you had not noticed before, such as the different tones, colors, textures, markings, and other elements—without any judgment.

- Write down at least 5 positive words to describe your skin. Look beyond your face and examine the rest of your skin.

- If you would like, draw your body and note the interesting or hardworking parts of your skin.

- What is special and remarkable about your skin? What do you appreciate about it?

# REFLECTION ZONE

- Jot down what you observed and noticed about yourself during today's activity. ....................................................................................

- What thoughts came up for you during this activity? ..............................

  ....................................................................................

- How did your body feel during this activity? (For examples, you can refer to the list on page 13.) ..........................................................

  ....................................................................................

- What feelings and emotions did you notice during this activity? (For examples, you can refer to the lists on pages 12–13.)

  ....................................................................................

- What did you learn about yourself that really stood out to you?

  ....................................................................................

- Did you find any parts of today's activity that you would like to keep as go-tos when you need to love the skin you are in? If so, jot down your keepers here: ..................................................................................

  ....................................................................................

- Jot down your word to carry with you to remind you how remarkable your skin is. ..................................................................................

## CHECKING IN WITH MYSELF AFTER EXPLORING TODAY'S ACTIVITY

**Circle the number below that describes how you are feeling right now.**

| 5=feeling really good now | 4=feeling good now | 3=feeling ok now | 2=not feeling good now | 1=really struggling now |

You explored this activity
and yourself—so cool!

## ACTIVITIES

Feeling Alone—It Happens

Mistakes Are So Human

When Hard Things Happen

# ADVENTURE #4:
## I Am Not Alone
## (Even When I Think I Am)

# FEELING ALONE—IT HAPPENS

Everyone sometimes feels down, sad, or all alone. The most important things to know when this happens are that this feeling will not last forever and you are not alone in feeling this way. It can be especially tough when you are young because often the social aspect of your life is extra important to you. You may feel rejected, as with a breakup, or excluded, perhaps from a personal pushback on social media. Some young people are hurting from being microaggressed over and over. In these situations, it is easy to feel like something is wrong with you—your inner critic might start to take control of your mind and convince you that it's your problem. When this happens, try to remember that you are not the only person who has felt this way—everyone has these experiences.

## ALONE IS NOT FOREVER

Today's activity will help you find some perspective and learn that feeling rejected or excluded, though painful, is also an invitation for you to be kinder and more compassionate toward yourself. It might offer an opportunity to find other ways of connecting with people who truly support you just as you are—and to remember that you do not need to be with people who are unkind, unhealthy, or harmful to you.

- Press your stop-and-notice button.

- Sit somewhere comfortable—really comfortable.

- Inhale and exhale slowly for 10 deep breaths, feeling or following each breath in and out.

- If there is any place on your body that may need some tender loving care, place a hand gently on that area and send it some love.

- Make a list of some ways that you can be kind to yourself when you might feel alone or excluded. Maybe you could listen to music that makes you feel good, or go for a nature walk, or play with a pet. Perhaps read a poem or meditate. (Do not scroll through a social media feed!)

- Next, make a list of some people you could connect with when you are feeling alone or excluded. Think about people who know and love you for who you are, people who bring out your best self, people who are comforting or wise.

- Write down some ways in which feeling alone can be a positive thing and not a sign that something is wrong.

# REFLECTION ZONE

- Jot down what you observed and noticed about yourself during today's activity............................................................................

- What thoughts came up for you during this activity?............................

  ................................................................................................................

- How did your body feel during this activity? (For examples, you can refer to the list on page 13.)...........................................................

  ................................................................................................................

- What feelings and emotions did you notice during this activity? (For examples, you can refer to the lists on pages 12–13.)

  ................................................................................................................

- What did you learn about yourself that really stood out to you?

  ................................................................................................................

- Did you find any parts of today's activity that you would like to keep as go-tos when you are feeling all alone or like you don't belong? If so, jot down your keepers here:.....................................................................

  ................................................................................................................

- Jot down your helpful word to carry with you when feeling alone or excluded............................................................................................

## CHECKING IN WITH MYSELF AFTER EXPLORING TODAY'S ACTIVITY

**Circle the number below that describes how you are feeling right now.**

| 5=feeling really good now | 4=feeling good now | 3=feeling ok now | 2=not feeling good now | 1=really struggling now |

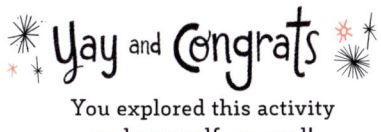

You explored this activity
and yourself—so cool!

# MISTAKES ARE SO HUMAN

## CHECKING IN WITH MYSELF BEFORE EXPLORING TODAY'S ACTIVITY

**Circle the number below that describes how you are feeling right now.**

5=feeling really good now     4=feeling good now     3=feeling ok now     2=not feeling good now     1=really struggling now

Making a mistake or failing at something feels totally awful! That wave of painful feelings can quickly push most young people over the edge. If it feels too terrible, you might even find yourself denying the situation. These reactions are human and normal, and they are unfortunately encouraged by a stream of messages from the world and on social media that emphasize perfection. Making a mistake, even a small one, can trigger a sense that you are bad or worthless or that something is really wrong with you. That is not true! Remember that literally everyone makes mistakes, and everyone is imperfect—being imperfect is something all humans share. So, you are not bad or incompetent when you make a mistake. You are just showing that you are fully human. The upside of mistakes is that you can learn from them. They tend to be excellent teachers if we slow down, don't judge, and mindfully reflect instead of panicking and feeling broken.

## MY IMPERFECT SELF

This activity is about recalling a recent personal mistake with kindness and insight because you are human—not a screwup.

- Press your stop-and-notice button.
- Sit somewhere comfortable—really comfortable.
- Inhale and exhale slowly for 10 deep breaths, feeling or following each breath in and out.
- If there is any place on your body that may need some tender loving care, place a hand gently on that area and send it some love.

- Briefly describe a recent mistake that you made.
- As you think about this situation, instead of being hard on yourself, think of yourself as being human, just like everyone else.
- Briefly describe what you learned from making this mistake.

# REFLECTION ZONE

- Jot down what you observed and noticed about yourself during today's activity......................................................................................................

- What thoughts came up for you during this activity?..............................

  ......................................................................................................

- How did your body feel during this activity? (For examples, you can refer to the list on page 13.) ........................................................................

  ......................................................................................................

- What feelings and emotions did you notice during this activity? (For examples, you can refer to the lists on pages 12–13.)

  ......................................................................................................

- What did you learn about yourself that really stood out to you?

  ......................................................................................................

- Did you find any parts of today's activity that you would like to keep as go-tos when you make a mistake? If so, jot down your keepers here:

  ......................................................................................................

- Jot down a word or phrase to carry with you to remind you that it is ok and human to make a mistake..................................................................

## CHECKING IN WITH MYSELF AFTER EXPLORING TODAY'S ACTIVITY

**Circle the number below that describes how you are feeling right now.**

| 5=feeling really good now | 4=feeling good now | 3=feeling ok now | 2=not feeling good now | 1=really struggling now |

You explored this activity
and yourself—so cool!

# WHEN HARD THINGS HAPPEN

You may be wondering how to stay calm when everything around you seems chaotic and over the top. Remember you are not alone in feeling out of control when this happens. One of the most effective things you can do is to notice and then try to mindfully name or write down the feelings and emotions that you are experiencing rather than ignoring them or trying to get rid of them. This is not always easy, but if you can describe your feelings and emotions while being self-compassionate, you will be able to view your experience with more kindness and self-support. (It's ok if you don't have the words—do your best, or consult the lists of feelings on pages 12–13 for some ideas.)

Self-compassion is all about responding to struggles, hard times, and pain with kindliness and tenderness. When you choose to be self-compassionate, you are mindfully paying attention to the hurt you are feeling, but with deep kindness toward your discomfort. Being self-compassionate is also about doing what you can to soothe and care for yourself rather than ignoring your uncomfortable feelings.

## RESPONDING TO DIFFICULT MOMENTS

This activity is an invitation to experiment with meeting your hard times with self-compassion rather than beating yourself up or ignoring your struggle.

- Press your stop-and-notice button.
- Sit somewhere comfortable—really comfortable.
- Inhale and exhale slowly for 10 deep breaths, feeling or following each breath in and out.

- If there is any place on your body that may need some tender loving care, place a hand gently on that area and send it some love.

- Think about a hard time you have gone through.

- Write about that hard time, and name the feelings and emotions that you experienced.

- Now think about several ways in which you could have expressed some compassion toward yourself during this hard time. Write down how you have shown some support or kindness toward yourself.

# REFLECTION ZONE

- Jot down what you observed and noticed about yourself during today's activity..............................................................................................

- What thoughts came up for you during this activity?.............................

.................................................................................................................

- How did your body feel during this activity? (For examples, you can refer to the list on page 13.)..........................................................................

.................................................................................................................

- What feelings and emotions did you notice during this activity? (For examples, you can refer to the lists on pages 12–13.)

.................................................................................................................

- What did you learn about yourself that really stood out to you?

.................................................................................................................

- Did you find any parts of today's activity that you would like to keep as go-tos when hard things happen and you need some self-compassion? If so, jot down your keepers here:..............................................................

.................................................................................................................

- Jot down a word or phrase to carry with you for when you go through a difficult experience.........................................................................................

## CHECKING IN WITH MYSELF AFTER EXPLORING TODAY'S ACTIVITY

**Circle the number below that describes how you are feeling right now.**

| 5=feeling really good now | 4=feeling good now | 3=feeling ok now | 2=not feeling good now | 1=really struggling now |

You explored this activity
and yourself—so cool!

## ACTIVITIES

My Social and Cultural Connections

My Inner Friend

What Do I Need Right Now?

Self-Kindness: Let Me Count the Ways

May I Be _____

My Gender Identity Ministory

# ADVENTURE #5:
## Self-Kindness
## (A New Way to Be Me)

# MY SOCIAL AND CULTURAL CONNECTIONS

Culture is a very important part of identity. Some people have many cultural identities that shape their day-to-day reality and the truth of who they are in the world. You may also have multiple social identities. Your cultural-social identities may be connected to race; ethnicity; gender identity, gender neutrality, or gender nonconformity; religion; age; social class; nationality; sexual orientation; neurotype; immigration status; ability; spirituality; language; personality; and many other qualities, characteristics, or interests. In the process of discovering all that and becoming an emotionally healthy adult, it is important to bring value and appreciation to your cultural and social identities.

## APPRECIATING MY IDENTITY

This activity is an invitation to truly celebrate your social and cultural identities.

- Press your stop-and-notice button.
- Sit very comfortably and close your eyes or drop your gaze downward.
- Inhale and exhale slowly for 10 deep breaths, feeling or following each breath in and out.
- If there is any place on your body that may need some tender loving care, place a hand gently on that area and send it some love.
- Make a list of all of your diverse cultural-social connections.
- Now, next to each item in your list, write down all the reasons that you love or are proud of each of your cultural-social connections.

# REFLECTION ZONE

- Jot down what you observed and noticed about yourself during today's activity.............................................................................................

- What thoughts came up for you during this activity?..............................

  ...........................................................................................................

- How did your body feel during this activity? (For examples, you can refer to the list on page 13.) .........................................................................

  ...........................................................................................................

- What feelings and emotions did you notice during this activity? (For examples, you can refer to the lists on pages 12–13.)

  ...........................................................................................................

- What did you learn about yourself that really stood out to you?

  ...........................................................................................................

- Did you find any parts of today's activity that you would like to keep as go-tos when you need to celebrate your social and cultural connections? If so, jot down your keepers here: ...............................................................

  ...........................................................................................................

- Jot down a word or phrase to carry with you that supports your social and cultural identities............................................................................................

## CHECKING IN WITH MYSELF AFTER EXPLORING TODAY'S ACTIVITY

**Circle the number below that describes how you are feeling right now.**

| 5=feeling really good now | 4=feeling good now | 3=feeling ok now | 2=not feeling good now | 1=really struggling now |

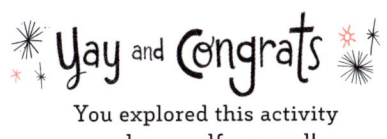

You explored this activity
and yourself—so cool!

# MY INNER FRIEND

It is so cool to have a best friend, especially when you need someone to talk with who truly understands you. Having a friend who is always there for you, anytime and anywhere, is a true gift. What if you could have that friend whenever you were in need? The way to do it is to be your own BFF. You can discover and connect to your own inner friend. Your inner friend is that part of you that is always available, compassionate, and supportive whenever you are struggling or harshly judging yourself. We all have this inner friend who is just waiting to care for us—but we have to practice bringing that friend to the forefront, instead of letting our inner critic take over the stage.

## FINDING MY INNER FRIEND

This activity will help you discover and connect with your inner friend. Practicing will make sure you can call on your inner friend whenever you need to.

- Sit very comfortably and close your eyes or drop your gaze downward.
- Begin to "feel" your current posture by noticing your lower body and then your upper body.
- Place one or two hands on your chest and feel the temperature of your palms.
- If you would like, begin to notice your breath—both inhalations and exhalations—for about one minute.
- Imagine a very kind and compassionate friend that you carry inside you. What would your friend look like? Draw or describe your friend.

- Give your inner friend a name and jot it down.

- Now write down the most helpful and kind things your inner friend would say to you when you are feeling down or struggling. (For example, "You are a great person and you will get through this," or "This hard time won't last forever," or "I know this hurts, but eventually you will be ok.")

- Now, read aloud each of the things that your inner friend would say to you 3 times.

# REFLECTION ZONE

- ◦ Jot down what you observed and noticed about yourself during today's activity..................................................................................................

- ◦ What thoughts came up for you during this activity? ...........................
..................................................................................................

- ◦ How did your body feel during this activity? (For examples, you can refer to the list on page 13.)...................................................................
..................................................................................................

- ◦ What feelings and emotions did you notice during this activity? (For examples, you can refer to the lists on pages 12–13.)
..................................................................................................

- ◦ What did you learn about yourself that really stood out to you?
..................................................................................................

- ◦ Did you find any parts of today's activity that you would like to keep as go-tos when you need your inner friend? If so, jot down your keepers here:........................................................................................
..................................................................................................

- ◦ Jot down the name of your inner friend to carry with you.
..................................................................................................

## CHECKING IN WITH MYSELF AFTER EXPLORING TODAY'S ACTIVITY

**Circle the number below that describes how you are feeling right now.**

| 5=feeling really good now | 4=feeling good now | 3=feeling ok now | 2=not feeling good now | 1=really struggling now |

**Yay and Congrats**

You explored this activity
and yourself—so cool!

# WHAT DO I NEED RIGHT NOW?

Now that you have connected with your self-compassionate inner friend, you can use this resource any time—if you are stressed, sad, or mad, know that your inner friend is always there waiting to support you. One excellent way to tap into your inner friend's helpfulness is to ask this question: "What do I really need to hear right now to help me get through this situation?" If you pause and really listen to your inner friend, you will very likely discover just what you need to do to feel better. The best way to practice self-compassion is to notice that you are struggling and have your inner friend respond by suggesting some healthy and comforting or active choices. It may not totally solve your issue, but it will help you to choose actions that are kind and wise instead of hasty or even self-destructive.

## LISTENING TO MY INNER FRIEND

This activity is about connecting to the part of you that can be relied upon to deliver kind words and suggest positive actions—your inner friend.

- Sit very comfortably and close your eyes or drop your gaze downward.

- Begin to "feel" your current posture by noticing your lower body and then your upper body.

- Place one or two hands on your chest and feel the temperature of your palms.

- If you would like, begin to notice your breath—both inhalations and exhalations—for about one minute.

- Call to mind a small or medium problem you experienced and write it down.

- Describe how you feel in your body when you think about this small or medium problem.

- Call on your inner friend by asking yourself these questions: "What did I really need to hear in that moment?" and "What could I do that would be positive for me?"

- Then, sit quietly, take a few slow, deep breaths, and just listen from your heart. Notice whatever advice, thoughts, and suggestions come up. As these arise, write them down.

# REFLECTION ZONE

- Jot down what you observed and noticed about yourself during today's activity........................................................................................

- What thoughts came up for you during this activity?...........................

  ........................................................................................

- How did your body feel during this activity? (For examples, you can refer to the list on page 13.) ........................................................

  ........................................................................................

- What feelings and emotions did you notice during this activity? (For examples, you can refer to the lists on pages 12–13.)

  ........................................................................................

- What did you learn about yourself that really stood out to you?

  ........................................................................................

- Did you find any parts of today's activity that you would like to keep as go-tos in order to understand what you really need right now? If so, jot down your keepers here:.......................................................

  ........................................................................................

- Jot down a word or phrase to remind you to really tune in to what you need.......................................................................................

## CHECKING IN WITH MYSELF AFTER EXPLORING TODAY'S ACTIVITY

**Circle the number below that describes how you are feeling right now.**

5=feeling really good now    4=feeling good now    3=feeling ok now    2=not feeling good now    1=really struggling now

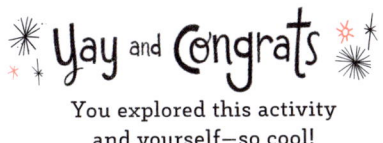

You explored this activity
and yourself—so cool!

# SELF-KINDNESS: LET ME COUNT THE WAYS

When it comes to practicing self-compassion, it really helps to make a personal list of ways that you can show kindness toward yourself. With a good list in hand, you always have a quick guide to refer to when you're feeling stressed or are about to react without thinking. This list can help you remember that you have a friend in yourself, that you can slow down and be mindful, and make thoughtful choices about how to respond to difficult situations. Your list of self-kindnesses can include things like taking a walk outdoors, listening and/or moving to music that feels uplifting, drinking a glass of water, talking to a friend, taking a moment to breathe, or whatever small act makes you feel good.

## MY SELF-KINDNESS LIST

This activity will help you create your own personal set of ways to practice self-kindness that you can draw upon at any time. You'll get better at understanding your needs in the moment and connecting with your inner friend.

- Sit very comfortably and close your eyes or drop your gaze downward.
- Begin to "feel" your current posture by noticing your lower body and then your upper body.
- Place one or two hands on your chest and feel the temperature of your palms.
- If you would like, begin to notice your breath—both inhalations and exhalations—for about one minute.
- Make a list of as many ways you can think of to show yourself kindness. This includes kindness toward your thoughts, body, feelings, emotions, stressors, and problems.

- Try to make a list of at least 12 acts of self-kindness. More would be even better!

- When you're done, make a copy of your list that you can post in your room, tuck into your bag, or keep on your phone—somewhere handy, so that you can quickly refer to it as needed.

# REFLECTION ZONE

- Jot down what you observed and noticed about yourself during today's activity. ........................................................................................

- What thoughts came up for you during this activity? ...........................

  ........................................................................................

- How did your body feel during this activity? (For examples, you can refer to the list on page 13.) .......................................................

  ........................................................................................

- What feelings and emotions did you notice during this activity? (For examples, you can refer to the lists on pages 12–13.)

  ........................................................................................

- What did you learn about yourself that really stood out to you?

  ........................................................................................

- Did you find any parts of today's activity that you would like to keep as go-tos when you need to show yourself an awesome act of kindness? If so, jot down your keepers here: .........................................................

  ........................................................................................

- Jot down a self-kindness word or phrase to carry with you.

  ........................................................................................

## CHECKING IN WITH MYSELF AFTER EXPLORING TODAY'S ACTIVITY

**Circle the number below that describes how you are feeling right now.**

| 5=feeling really good now | 4=feeling good now | 3=feeling ok now | 2=not feeling good now | 1=really struggling now |

You explored this activity
and yourself—so cool!

# MAY I BE _____

It is time to bring your imagination into play in how you think about yourself. Now that you have some practice treating yourself with kindness, this is a great moment for you to draw upon your heart and soul to connect to a positive, healthy wish you have for yourself. Think of something beautiful that you want, desire, or dream of for yourself. What an amazing way to bring some kindness to yourself! It may even power up your wish and help it to come true. The sky is the limit, so do not restrict your imagination—dream big or small, but dream detailed, and dream up a true and wonderful vision of what could be!

## MY WISH FOR MYSELF

This activity is an invitation to imagine and identify a positive, healthy personal wish.

- Sit very comfortably and close your eyes or drop your gaze downward.

- Begin to "feel" your current posture by noticing your lower body and then your upper body.

- Place one or two hands on your chest and feel the temperature of your palms.

- If you would like, begin to notice your breath—both inhalations and exhalations—for about one minute.

- Slowly read or say the following phrase out loud 5 or 6 times: "May I be _____ ."

- Then, focus inward on your body and your heart, and notice what ideas come up to fill in the blank that are healthy and positive.

- Write down what you imagined for yourself.

# REFLECTION ZONE

- Jot down what you observed and noticed about yourself during today's activity...................................................................................

- What thoughts came up for you during this activity?...........................

....................................................................................................

- How did your body feel during this activity? (For examples, you can refer to the list on page 13.) .......................................................

....................................................................................................

- What feelings and emotions did you notice during this activity? (For examples, you can refer to the lists on pages 12-13.)

....................................................................................................

- What did you learn about yourself that really stood out to you?

....................................................................................................

- Did you find any parts of today's activity that you would like to keep as go-tos in order to help you imagine something positive for your future? If so, jot down your keepers here:...............................................

....................................................................................................

- Jot down the words you used to fill in the blank as you focused on today and beyond.....................................................................................

## CHECKING IN WITH MYSELF AFTER EXPLORING TODAY'S ACTIVITY

**Circle the number below that describes how you are feeling right now.**

| 5=feeling really good now | 4=feeling good now | 3=feeling ok now | 2=not feeling good now | 1=really struggling now |

You explored this activity
and yourself—so cool!

# MY GENDER IDENTITY MINISTORY

Although gender identity is expansive and fluid in many ways, we all have a gender expression that is a big part of who we are and how we show ourselves to the world. A young person's gender identity has a great deal of importance and meaning. Have you ever thought about the way you identify in a gendered way—and how it has influenced you from the inside out? And have you thought about this gender identity with self-compassion? If not, you will finally have your turn now.

## MY GENDER IDENTITY

This activity will offer you the opportunity to explore your own sense of gender identity with self-compassion.

- Sit very comfortably and close your eyes or drop your gaze downward.
- Begin to "feel" your current posture by noticing your lower body and then your upper body.
- Place one or two hands on your chest and feel the temperature of your palms.
- If you would like, begin to notice your breath—both inhalations and exhalations—for about one minute.
- Write or draw a ministory about your own gender identity and what it means to you. You can jot down memories and hopes, or sketch how you interpret your gender identity.
- Be open and kind to yourself as you explore these ideas; call upon your inner friend as you write.

## REFLECTION ZONE

- Jot down what you observed and noticed about yourself during today's activity. .............................................................................................

- What thoughts came up for you during this activity? ...............................
  .............................................................................................

- How did your body feel during this activity? (For examples, you can refer to the list on page 13.) .............................................................
  .............................................................................................

- What feelings and emotions did you notice during this activity? (For examples, you can refer to the lists on pages 12–13.)
  .............................................................................................

- What did you learn about yourself that really stood out to you?
  .............................................................................................

- Did you find any parts of today's activity that you would like to keep as go-tos when you think about your gender identity? ...............................
  .............................................................................................

- Jot down a word or phrase that gives you a positive feeling about your gender identity. .............................................................................

## CHECKING IN WITH MYSELF AFTER EXPLORING TODAY'S ACTIVITY

**Circle the number below that describes how you are feeling right now.**

| 5=feeling really good now | 4=feeling good now | 3=feeling ok now | 2=not feeling good now | 1=really struggling now |

You explored this activity
and yourself—so cool!

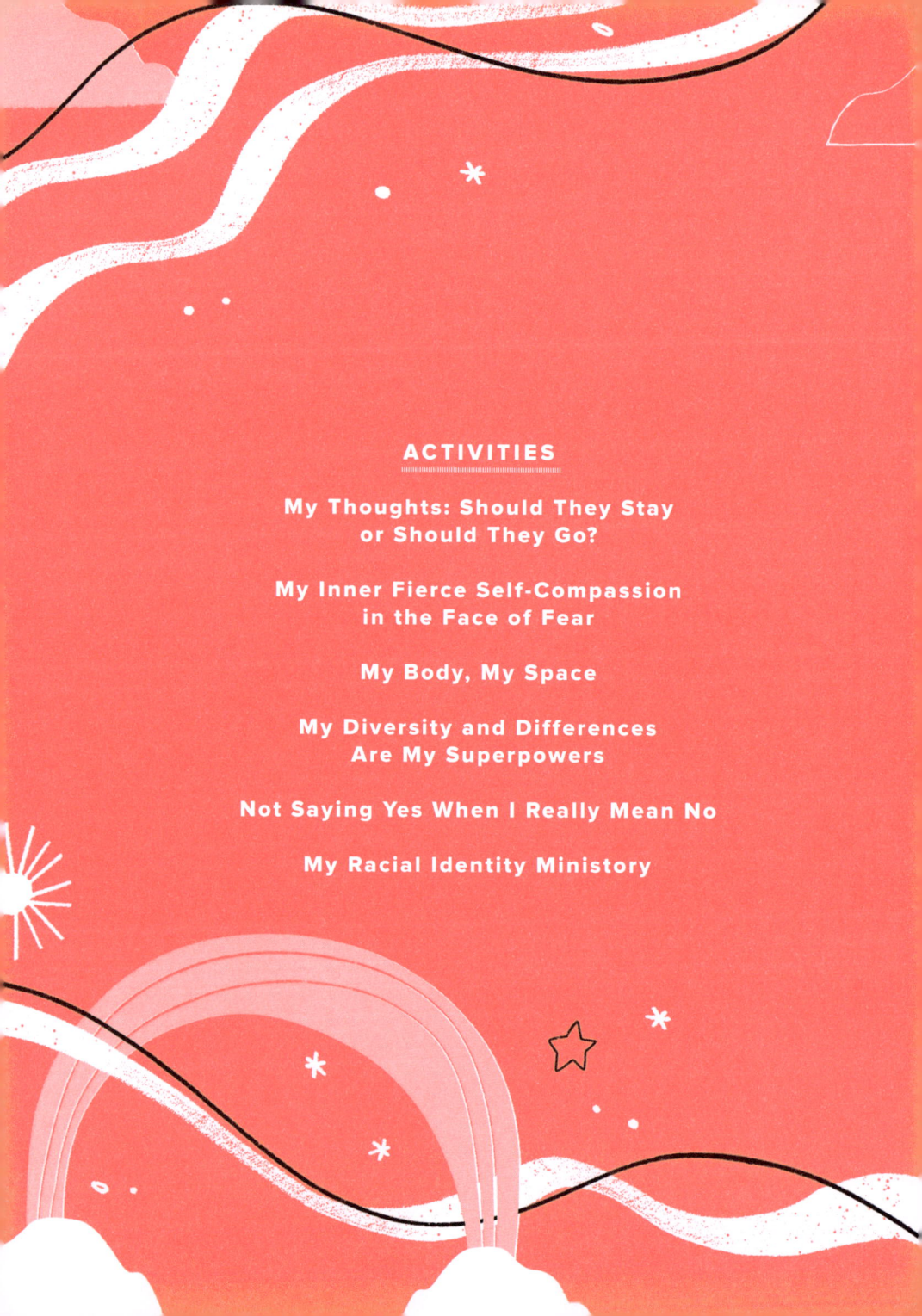

## ACTIVITIES

My Thoughts: Should They Stay
or Should They Go?

My Inner Fierce Self-Compassion
in the Face of Fear

My Body, My Space

My Diversity and Differences
Are My Superpowers

Not Saying Yes When I Really Mean No

My Racial Identity Ministory

# ADVENTURE #6:
## Fierce Self-Compassion for Taking Smart Action

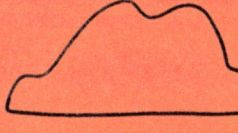

# MY THOUGHTS: SHOULD THEY STAY OR SHOULD THEY GO?

## CHECKING IN WITH MYSELF BEFORE EXPLORING TODAY'S ACTIVITY

**Circle the number below that describes how you are feeling right now.**

| 5=feeling really good now | 4=feeling good now | 3=feeling ok now | 2=not feeling good now | 1=really struggling now |

By now you are comfortable with the notion that your ideas can be wildly inaccurate at times and also that thoughts and feelings are not permanent. You might be growing more curious about how your thoughts can be helpful or not helpful to you. You have the power to make "thought choices." You can hold onto thoughts that are worthy of your attention and you can let go of self-critical or harmful thoughts. The thoughts that are moving you toward healthy choices and taking smart actions are the ones you want to hold onto. If you have thoughts that are pushing you away from being healthy and leading you to unwise actions, you can choose to release them so they can move into the departure lounge and go away!

## RECOGNIZING MY POSITIVE AND NEGATIVE THOUGHTS

This activity is about bringing curiosity to how your thoughts affect your choices, with the goal of practicing holding on to your healthy, positivity-inducing thoughts while letting unhealthy, self-damaging thoughts move on.

- Sit comfortably and close your eyes or drop your gaze downward.

- Begin to "feel" your current posture: notice your lower body and then your upper body.

- Place one or two hands on your chest and feel the weight and temperature of your palms for a few moments.

- If you would like, begin to notice your breath, following both inhalations and exhalations for about one minute.

- Think of a recent small- or medium-intensity struggle you went through.

- Make a list of all the different thoughts that came up during this struggle.
- Jot down the feelings and emotions that were connected to this struggle.
- Jot down any sensations you may have felt in your body.
- Be curious about each thought that you wrote down. Was it a helpful thought or a harmful thought?
- Then, become the commander of the thoughts you listed: write next to each thought *H* for healthy or *U* for unhealthy.
- Describe how the *H* thoughts led or might have led you toward taking smart action and how the *U* thoughts might have moved you away from taking smart action.

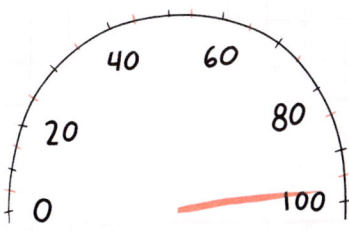

# REFLECTION ZONE

- Jot down what you observed and noticed about yourself during today's activity.........................................................................................

- What thoughts came up for you during this activity?.............................

.......................................................................................................

- How did your body feel during this activity? (For examples, you can refer to the list on page 13.) ........................................................

.......................................................................................................

- What feelings and emotions did you notice during this activity? (For examples, you can refer to the lists on pages 12–13.)

.......................................................................................................

- What did you learn about yourself that really stood out to you?

.......................................................................................................

- Did you find any parts of today's activity that you would like to keep as go-tos when you need to choose the thoughts that are helpful vs. unhelpful? If so, jot down your keepers here:...................................

.......................................................................................................

- Jot down a word that will help you remember to choose your keeper thoughts wisely.......................................................................................

## CHECKING IN WITH MYSELF AFTER EXPLORING TODAY'S ACTIVITY

**Circle the number below that describes how you are feeling right now.**

| 5=feeling really good now | 4=feeling good now | 3=feeling ok now | 2=not feeling good now | 1=really struggling now |

You explored this activity
and yourself—so cool!

# MY INNER FIERCE SELF-COMPASSION IN THE FACE OF FEAR

## CHECKING IN WITH MYSELF BEFORE EXPLORING TODAY'S ACTIVITY

**Circle the number below that describes how you are feeling right now.**

| 5=feeling really good now | 4=feeling good now | 3=feeling ok now | 2=not feeling good now | 1=really struggling now |
|---|---|---|---|---|

There is no doubt that there are things in life that are frightening because they are truly unsafe: you need to avoid them and the harm they can cause. On the other hand, there are also things that may scare us because they are new or different, but that actually turn out to be good for us, from trying a new food or activity to applying for a job that we want but may not feel ready for. Take a moment to think about the difference between fear of the truly unsafe and fear of expanding your horizons. Often, the things we fear are in some ways invitations to get out of our comfort zone. But when confronted with something scary, our minds typically don't analyze the thing that scared us—more often we just come up with a host of reasons not to face whatever prompted the feeling of fear. This is a time when your inner "fierce" self-compassion can come to your assistance to help you decide whether and how to deal with a fear.

## FACING MY FEARS

This activity is about recognizing and responding to expansive fears—the ones that prevent us from expanding our capacities—with fierce self-compassion, which is all about motivating and protecting ourselves, so that we are able to take the actions we need despite the fears we feel.

- Sit comfortably and close your eyes or drop your gaze downward.
- Begin to "feel" your current posture: notice your lower body and then your upper body.
- Place one or two hands on your chest and feel the weight and temperature of your palms for a few moments.

- If you would like, begin to notice your breath, following both inhalations and exhalations for about one minute.

- Call to mind an expansive fear that you have—not an unsafe fear.

- Describe in writing or sketch a simple picture of your fear.

- Jot down any other feelings and emotions attached to this fear.

- Jot down where you tend to feel this particular fear in your body.

- Jot down your wild-mind thoughts about your fear.

- Now think about and write down what the inner fierce self-compassionate and motivating part of you would say to you and to your wild mind about this expansive fear.

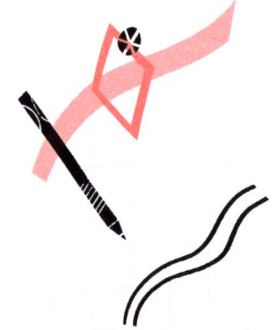

# REFLECTION ZONE

- Jot down what you observed and noticed about yourself during today's activity. ........................................................................................................

- What thoughts came up for you during this activity?.............................

  ........................................................................................................

- How did your body feel during this activity? (For examples, you can refer to the list on page 13.) ........................................................................

  ........................................................................................................

- What feelings and emotions did you notice during this activity? (For examples, you can refer to the lists on pages 12–13.)

  ........................................................................................................

- What did you learn about yourself that really stood out to you?

  ........................................................................................................

- Did you find any parts of today's activity that you would like to keep as go-tos when you want to meet an expansive fear with fierce self-compassion? If so, jot down your keepers here: ....................................

  ........................................................................................................

- Jot down a word that will help you access the fierce self-compassionate part of you...............................................................................................

## CHECKING IN WITH MYSELF AFTER EXPLORING TODAY'S ACTIVITY

**Circle the number below that describes how you are feeling right now.**

| 5=feeling really good now | 4=feeling good now | 3=feeling ok now | 2=not feeling good now | 1=really struggling now |

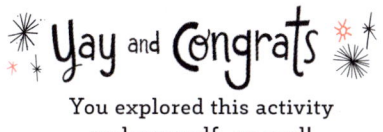

**You explored this activity and yourself—so cool!**

# MY BODY, MY SPACE

Sometimes your body may tell you "I need more space." These are moments when you need a measure of distance from other people, places, or situations to feel comfortable. Other times you may require less distance and more closeness to feel safe. These feelings are your body's way of protecting you by creating boundaries. When you are physically too close to questionable people or situations, you will most likely feel uncomfortable; when you are physically too isolated from people or places where you feel safe, you may experience a similar discomfort. Fierce self-compassion can be super helpful in protecting your body and yourself in these situations. Your mindful awareness of this bodily discomfort can connect to your fierce self-compassion's protective expression by prompting you to speak up and/or move to your desired degree of distance or closeness.

## FINDING MY SPACE

This activity is an opportunity to experiment with body boundaries and your inner self-compassionate voice. It is designed to help you create and keep a healthy distance in any situation.

- Sit comfortably and close your eyes or drop your gaze downward.
- Begin to "feel" your current posture: notice your lower body and then your upper body.
- Place one or two hands on your chest and feel the weight and temperature of your palms for a few moments.
- If you would like, begin to notice your breath, following both inhalations and exhalations for about one minute.

- Write about people, places, and situations that make you feel comfortable with more personal body closeness.

- Then, describe the people, places, and situations that make you more comfortable with a greater degree of space and distance.

- Reflect upon and jot down how your inner fierce self-compassionate protectiveness may signal to you that your body boundaries are out of balance and need some adjustment.

- Finally, write down how you can get the comfortable distance you need. What can you say or do? Practice saying something out loud or moving yourself to a more comfortable distance.

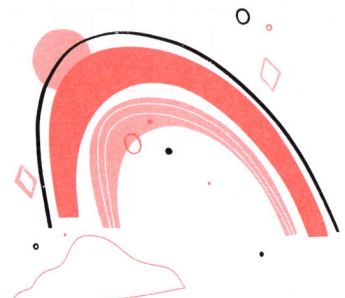

# REFLECTION ZONE

- Jot down what you observed and noticed about yourself during today's activity. ........................................................................................................

- What thoughts came up for you during this activity? .............................

  ........................................................................................................

- How did your body feel during this activity? (For examples, you can refer to the list on page 13.) ......................................................................

  ........................................................................................................

- What feelings and emotions did you notice during this activity? (For examples, you can refer to the lists on pages 12–13.)

  ........................................................................................................

- What did you learn about yourself that really stood out to you?

  ........................................................................................................

- Did you find any parts of today's activity that you would like to keep as go-tos whenever you need to change the body space you're in? If so, jot down your keepers here: ..........................................................................

  ........................................................................................................

- Jot down a word or phrase that will help you take action when you need more or less space. ........................................................................................

## CHECKING IN WITH MYSELF AFTER EXPLORING TODAY'S ACTIVITY

**Circle the number below that describes how you are feeling right now.**

5=feeling really good now   4=feeling good now   3=feeling ok now   2=not feeling good now   1=really struggling now

You explored this activity and yourself—so cool!

# MY DIVERSITY AND DIFFERENCES ARE MY SUPERPOWERS

## CHECKING IN WITH MYSELF BEFORE EXPLORING TODAY'S ACTIVITY

**Circle the number below that describes how you are feeling right now.**

| 5=feeling really good now | 4=feeling good now | 3=feeling ok now | 2=not feeling good now | 1=really struggling now |

We all have multifaceted cultural and social identities in the world. Some of these identities come with certain automatic social advantages; those advantages also confer disadvantages on those who do not share them. Sadly, the dominant people in many societies typically make up false narratives or stories to justify which groups are at the top of the social ladder and which groups are at the bottom. There is no truth behind these narratives: it is simply false that certain people are bad or not valuable, and it is wrong for these people to be negatively "othered" due to their identity. Sadly, these untruths have been around so long that they have been strongly absorbed into just about all social systems. That means that if you identify with any of the less advantaged social identities, you have experienced a different day-to-day reality than members of the advantaged group. How can you sensitively respond to yourself and the world if you identify with any of the cultural and social disadvantaged identities?

## TAPPING INTO MY SUPERPOWERS

The thing to remember is that these nondominant identities have been created by false stories. However, you can push back. You can take charge and reverse out of the false stories about who you are—and instead, you can opt into the truth of you. Your unique identity is actually your real superpower. This activity is designed to help you recognize your superpowers.

- Sit comfortably and close your eyes or drop your gaze downward.
- Begin to "feel" your current posture: notice your lower body and then your upper body.

- Place one or two hands on your chest and feel the weight and temperature of your palms for a few moments.

- If you would like, begin to notice your breath, following both inhalations and exhalations for about one minute.

- If you wish, move your body in a way that represents your cultural identities in motion for a few moments.

- List all the cultural and social identities of disadvantage that you personally connect with. If you do not have any disadvantaged identities, pick someone who does and use your compassionate imagination for this activity.

- Describe your feelings about your cultural-social identities.

- Think of some ways that you can "flip" the false stories about the meaning of your cultural-social identities to create a true ministory that shows your uniqueness, courage, and strength.

- Share your superpowers ministory here.

# REFLECTION ZONE

○ Jot down what you observed and noticed about yourself during today's activity. ........................................................................................

○ What thoughts came up for you during this activity? ...........................
........................................................................................................

○ How did your body feel during this activity? (For examples, you can refer to the list on page 13.) ...........................................................
........................................................................................................

○ What feelings and emotions did you notice during this activity? (For examples, you can refer to the lists on pages 12–13.)
........................................................................................................

○ What did you learn about yourself that really stood out to you?
........................................................................................................

○ Did you find any parts of today's activity that you would like to keep as go-tos whenever you need to call upon your social and cultural identity-based superpowers? If so, jot down your keepers here: ...........................
........................................................................................................

○ Jot down a word to carry with you that will remind you of your social and cultural superpowers. ...........................................................................

## CHECKING IN WITH MYSELF AFTER EXPLORING TODAY'S ACTIVITY

**Circle the number below that describes how you are feeling right now.**

| 5=feeling really good now | 4=feeling good now | 3=feeling ok now | 2=not feeling good now | 1=really struggling now |

You explored this activity
and yourself—so cool!

# NOT SAYING YES WHEN I REALLY MEAN NO

## CHECKING IN WITH MYSELF BEFORE EXPLORING TODAY'S ACTIVITY

**Circle the number below that describes how you are feeling right now.**

| 5=feeling really good now | 4=feeling good now | 3=feeling ok now | 2=not feeling good now | 1=really struggling now |
|---|---|---|---|---|

One way of showing fierce self-compassion is by standing up for yourself. Especially for young people, it can feel too easy to say yes to certain things because you want to be a part of a group, an activity, or to feel like you truly belong with your friends, team, or coworkers. It is totally normal to respond this way. Yet, this "people-pleasing" urge can easily get out of bounds or become a habit, and you end up saying yes to things that you don't truly want to do. First, know that you do not have to go along with others when they expect you to do or say things that make you feel uncomfortable or are even harmful. You can still be social while having your own limits; fierce self-protection will help you to say no. Second, you do not have to do things that you do not want to do, even if there is nothing problematic about the request other than it not matching up with what you want.

## TEACHING MYSELF TO SAY NO

This activity is about stepping up your practice of fierce self-compassion by learning to set important social self-protective limits and say yes only when you really mean it.

- Sit comfortably and close your eyes or drop your gaze downward.

- Begin to "feel" your current posture: notice your lower body and then your upper body.

- Place one or two hands on your chest and feel the weight and temperature of your palms for a few moments.

- If you would like, begin to notice your breath, following both inhalations and exhalations for about one minute.

- List all the people-pleasing, potentially uncomfortable, and actually harmful social things that you might be asked to do.

- Write down a script for saying no to each thing, such as "Thank you for asking, but I'm not free that evening," or "Thanks, but that won't work for me," or, simply, "No, thanks."

- Practice your script so you are comfortable with the words; this practice will help you to not automatically blurt out a yes that you regret.

## REFLECTION ZONE

- Jot down what you observed and noticed about yourself during today's activity.................................................................................................
- What thoughts came up for you during this activity?..............................
....................................................................................................................
- How did your body feel during this activity? (For examples, you can refer to the list on page 13.) ................................................................
....................................................................................................................
- What feelings and emotions did you notice during this activity? (For examples, you can refer to the lists on pages 12-13.)
....................................................................................................................
- What did you learn about yourself that really stood out to you?
....................................................................................................................
- Did you find any parts of today's activity that you would like to keep as go-tos when you really need to say no? If so, jot down your keepers here:
....................................................................................................................
- Jot down any reminder words that will help you avoid saying yes when you don't truly want to..........................................................................
....................................................................................................................

## CHECKING IN WITH MYSELF AFTER EXPLORING TODAY'S ACTIVITY

**Circle the number below that describes how you are feeling right now.**

| 5=feeling really good now | 4=feeling good now | 3=feeling ok now | 2=not feeling good now | 1=really struggling now |

**Yay and Congrats**
You explored this activity
and yourself—so cool!

# MY RACIAL IDENTITY MINISTORY

Everyone has a racial identity. In white-dominant societies, most people of color have to be far more aware of their racial identity than those who identify as white. People of color must also contend with racism. This is the result of historical false-hoods that lower the social status of people with darker skin tones in comparison to those with white-appearing skin. This immense social injustice still prevails today. Because of this situation, we all have some kind of racial identity story that shapes our experiences in this world.

When we truly understand the injustice in our society, we begin to feel a deep need for social justice in the world. Standing up for social justice is also about standing up for self-justice. Self-compassion also means compassion for those around you.

## REFLECTING ON MY RACIAL IDENTITY

This activity is an invitation to reflect upon your sense of racial identity, in your world and in relation to others. It is also a chance to think about how you can express your sense of social justice.

- Sit comfortably and close your eyes or drop your gaze downward.
- Begin to "feel" your current posture: notice your lower body and then your upper body.
- Place one or two hands on your chest and feel the weight and temperature of your palms for a few moments.
- If you would like, begin to notice your breath, following both inhalations and exhalations for about one minute.

- If you wish, move your body in a way that represents your cultural identities in motion for a few moments.

- Reflect upon the race you identify with and what it means to you.

- Write a ministory about the very first time you learned about your own racial identity. How did this experience affect you?

- What does your racial identity mean to you today?

- How does your racial identity affect your relationship to the world around you?

- Describe your thoughts and feelings about self-justice and how you relate to social justice issues.

# REFLECTION ZONE

- Jot down what you observed and noticed about yourself during today's activity........................................................................................
- What thoughts came up for you during this activity?............................
  ........................................................................................
- How did your body feel during this activity? (For examples, you can refer to the list on page 13.) ............................................................
  ........................................................................................
- What feelings and emotions did you notice during this activity? (For examples, you can refer to the lists on pages 12–13.)
  ........................................................................................
- What did you learn about yourself that really stood out to you?
  ........................................................................................
- Did you find any parts of today's activity that you would like to keep as go-tos when you reflect upon your racial identity? If so, jot down your keepers here:............................................................................
- Jot down a word that connects to your racial identity............................
  ........................................................................................

## CHECKING IN WITH MYSELF AFTER EXPLORING TODAY'S ACTIVITY

**Circle the number below that describes how you are feeling right now.**

5=feeling really good now    4=feeling good now    3=feeling ok now    2=not feeling good now    1=really struggling now

**Yay and Congrats**

**You explored this activity and yourself—so cool!**

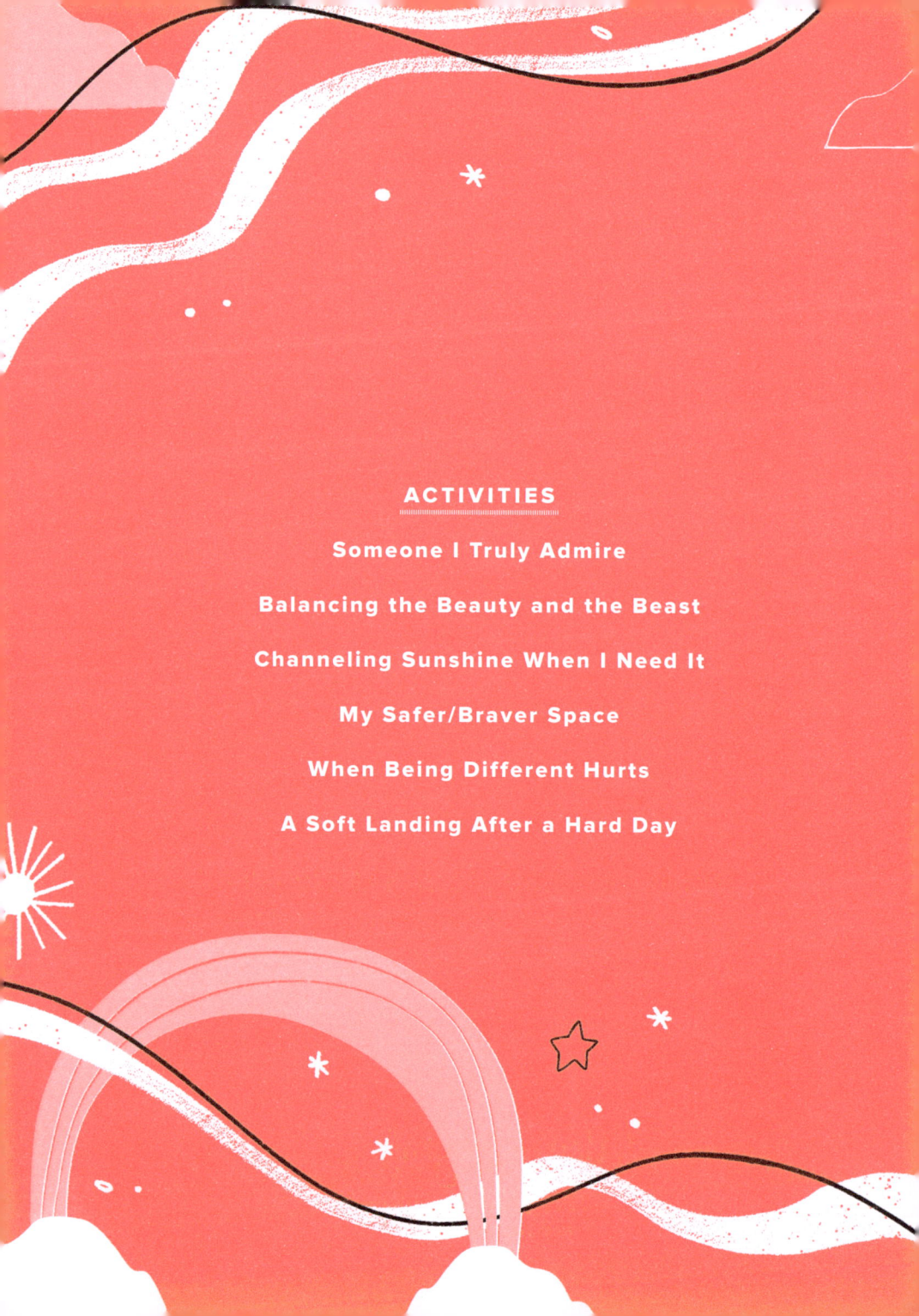

## ACTIVITIES

Someone I Truly Admire

Balancing the Beauty and the Beast

Channeling Sunshine When I Need It

My Safer/Braver Space

When Being Different Hurts

A Soft Landing After a Hard Day

# ADVENTURE #7:
## Practicing Self-Compassion When Feeling Mad, Sad, or Bad

# SOMEONE I TRULY ADMIRE

Having a role model is a great way to motivate yourself. Your role model could be someone you know or someone you've never met; an ancestor, a friend or family member, someone accomplished or famous, or even a fictional character—as long as it is someone who expresses the values and positive ways of being that you truly admire. Having a role model can be a self-compassionate and supportive resource in multiple ways—not only as an overall inspiration, but in the moment. For example, when you're feeling unsure of yourself or your choices, you might ask yourself what your role model would do in this situation or what they might say to you.

## MY ROLE MODEL

This activity is about identifying a positive role model that you can look to as a self-compassionate resource to help you be your best self.

- Get comfortable in the space and place you are in right now.
- Slowly breathe in for 3 counts and breathe out for 5 counts for one minute.
- If it would feel good to you, stretch or move your body for a few moments. Just give your body what it may need right now.
- Write down the name of someone you respect and could see as a role model.
- Now, write down or draw a picture of the qualities or accomplishments you really admire about this person.

- Write down how you might personally express or emulate any of your role model's positive traits. In what ways might these acts be self-compassionate?

- It's ok to have more than one role model for different aspects of your life; repeat the exercise for each one.

# REFLECTION ZONE

- Jot down what you observed and noticed about yourself during today's activity. ....................................................................................

- What thoughts came up for you during this activity?..........................
  ....................................................................................

- How did your body feel during this activity? (For examples, you can refer to the list on page 13.) ........................................................
  ....................................................................................

- What feelings and emotions did you notice during this activity? (For examples, you can refer to the lists on pages 12-13.)
  ....................................................................................

- What did you learn about yourself that really stood out to you?
  ....................................................................................

- Did you find any parts of today's activity that you would like to keep as go-tos when you need to express some of your role model's positive traits? If so jot down your keepers here: ..............................................
  ....................................................................................

- Jot down a word or short phrase that describes your role model.
  ....................................................................................

## CHECKING IN WITH MYSELF AFTER EXPLORING TODAY'S ACTIVITY

**Circle the number below that describes how you are feeling right now.**

| 5=feeling really good now | 4=feeling good now | 3=feeling ok now | 2=not feeling good now | 1=really struggling now |

You explored this activity
and yourself—so cool!

# BALANCING THE BEAUTY AND THE BEAST

Getting stuck in negativity is all too easy. Often when one thing goes wrong, it can seem like *everything* is wrong. It might feel like a horrible beast has invaded and ruined your space and plans to stay forever. When you feel this way, self-compassion can help by reminding you to remember all the beautiful things that are still right there where you live. Every good thing in your life adds up—even (and especially) the smaller stuff. Being kind to yourself by enjoying the simple beauty around you rather than focusing on the negative "beast" is one of the most effective ways to deal with negativity. Making a habit of giving your attention to the good things in your life is how you can continue to roll with the bitter and the sweet.

## FINDING THE BEAUTY

This activity is about bringing more balance to your times of negativity by mindfully focusing on the truly good and simply beautiful things around you.

- Get comfortable in the space and place you are in right now.
- Slowly breathe in for 3 counts and breathe out for 5 counts for one minute.
- If it would feel good to you, stretch or move your body for a few moments. Just give your body what it may need right now.
- Begin to pay mindful attention to the space you are in right now. Focus on all the things in your space that are good and beautiful. Feel free to go outside for this activity if you would like.
- Write down all the good and beautiful things that you noticed.
- Jot down how thinking about these things could make you feel better or more balanced the next time you are feeling down or negative.

# REFLECTION ZONE

- Jot down what you observed and noticed about yourself during today's activity. ..........................................................................................................

- What thoughts came up for you during this activity? ...........................
  ..........................................................................................................

- How did your body feel during this activity? (For examples, you can refer to the list on page 13.) ......................................................................
  ..........................................................................................................

- What feelings and emotions did you notice during this activity? (For examples, you can refer to the lists on pages 12–13.)
  ..........................................................................................................

- What did you learn about yourself that really stood out to you?
  ..........................................................................................................

- Did you find any parts of today's activity that you would like to keep as go-tos when you need to balance out your negativity? If so, jot down your keepers here: ...........................................................................................
  ..........................................................................................................

- Jot down a word or short phrase to carry with you to help you focus on the beauty instead of the beast. ...................................................................
  ..........................................................................................................

## CHECKING IN WITH MYSELF AFTER EXPLORING TODAY'S ACTIVITY

**Circle the number below that describes how you are feeling right now.**

| 5=feeling really good now | 4=feeling good now | 3=feeling ok now | 2=not feeling good now | 1=really struggling now |

**You explored this activity and yourself—so cool!**

# CHANNELING SUNSHINE WHEN I NEED IT

Feelings and emotions are like the weather—they come and they go. This is nature's way of teaching us that things constantly change in life, including how you may feel at any given moment. One day your interior weather might be warm and sunny, and the very next day it might be storming inside your heart, mind, and soul. When you know and accept that your emotions—even the most intense, sad, and bad ones—will not last forever, you know that eventually you will feel better, and the sun will reappear, just like your feelings of hope and peace.

## MY EMOTIONAL WEATHER REPORT

This exercise is designed to help build tools so that you can hang on and try to go with the flow of life and the flow of your feelings, no matter what kind of emotional weather you're experiencing.

- Get comfortable in the space and place you are in right now.

- Slowly breathe in for 3 counts and breathe out for 5 counts for one minute.

- If it would feel good to you, stretch or move your body for a few moments. Just give your body what it may need right now.

- If you are able, take a brief walk outside; alternatively, if you can, simply look outside and observe what's going on in nature.

- Mindfully press your stop-and-notice button, then direct your attention to how different parts of nature may be teaching you to notice change (observe the weather, watch the sky, notice the wind, look at any animals, trees, and other plants).

- Write about your experience of noticing the ebb and flow of nature.

- How might nature help you compassionately respond when you are feeling sad or bad or other unpleasant or uncomfortable emotions?

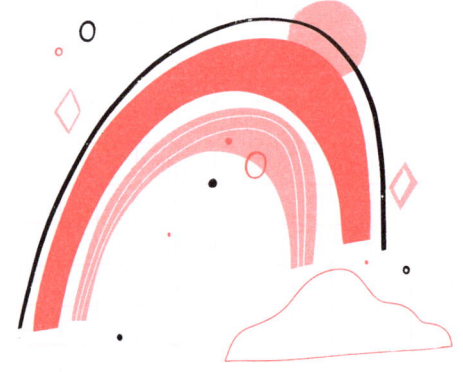

# REFLECTION ZONE

- Jot down what you observed and noticed about yourself during today's activity. .................................................................................................

- What thoughts came up for you during this activity? ..............................
.................................................................................................

- How did your body feel during this activity? (For examples, you can refer to the list on page 13.) ..........................................................
.................................................................................................

- What feelings and emotions did you notice during this activity? (For examples, you can refer to the lists on pages 12–13.)
.................................................................................................

- What did you learn about yourself that really stood out to you?
.................................................................................................

- Did you find any parts of today's activity that you would like to keep as go-tos when you are feeling sad or bad? If so, jot down your keepers here: .............................................................................................

- Jot down your "go with the flow" word to carry with you.

.................................................................................................

## CHECKING IN WITH MYSELF AFTER EXPLORING TODAY'S ACTIVITY

**Circle the number below that describes how you are feeling right now.**

5=feeling really good now    4=feeling good now    3=feeling ok now    2=not feeling good now    1=really struggling now

You explored this activity
and yourself—so cool!

# MY SAFER/BRAVER SPACE

A very helpful resource for being self-compassionate is a space of your own, a place where you can feel safe and find your courage. I call this your "safer/braver space." It can be a physical, IRL place or it can be an imaginary headspace that you can visit in your mind. Wherever it is, your safer/braver space is a sweet spot, somewhere that is totally comfortable and reflects you. It is a soft place to fall when you need some chill-out time or tender loving care. It is also a space where you can land emotionally and reconnect with your best self so that you can feel safer and braver when it is time to go back to the world. Your self-compassion space can be anywhere that works for you—a comfy chair, your bed covered in pillows, your favorite blanket, a yoga mat, a cozy corner of the room, a cheery view out the window, or an imaginary space in your mind.

## DESIGNING MY NEST

This activity is about designing your own self-compassionate safer/braver space—your personal "nest"—with the elements that support you, and learning to visit it whenever you need it.

- Get comfortable in the space and place you are in right now.

- Slowly breathe in for 3 counts and breathe out for 5 counts for one minute.

- If it would feel good to you, stretch or move your body for a few moments. Just give your body what it may need right now.

- List some of your most cherished personal comfort items and/or any materials that make you feel relaxed, safe, and brave. These are what you will use to build your "nest." Feel free to list things such as blankets, pillows, books, signs, this journal, and any other favorite things for this project.

- If it works better for you, instead of a physical location, imagine a place where you would feel safer and braver. What would this place look like? You can always reimagine and configure this mental space as needed.

- Describe or draw your safer/braver space in detail.

- Whether you space is physical or mental, imagine yourself there. How does it feel?

# REFLECTION ZONE

- Jot down what you observed and noticed about yourself during today's activity......................................................................................

- What thoughts came up for you during this activity?............................

  ......................................................................................

- How did your body feel during this activity? (For examples, you can refer to the list on page 13.) .........................................................

  ......................................................................................

- What feelings and emotions did you notice during this activity? (For examples, you can refer to the lists on pages 12–13.)

  ......................................................................................

- What did you learn about yourself that really stood out to you?

  ......................................................................................

- Did you find any parts of today's activity that you would like to keep as go-tos when you need your safer/braver space? If so, jot down your keepers here:.......................................................................

  ......................................................................................

- Jot down a word that describes your safer/braver space so you can bring it to mind whenever you need it.................................................

## CHECKING IN WITH MYSELF AFTER EXPLORING TODAY'S ACTIVITY

**Circle the number below that describes how you are feeling right now.**

| 5=feeling really good now | 4=feeling good now | 3=feeling ok now | 2=not feeling good now | 1=really struggling now |

You explored this activity
and yourself—so cool!

# WHEN BEING DIFFERENT HURTS

## CHECKING IN WITH MYSELF BEFORE EXPLORING TODAY'S ACTIVITY

**Circle the number below that describes how you are feeling right now.**

| 5=feeling really good now | 4=feeling good now | 3=feeling ok now | 2=not feeling good now | 1=really struggling now |

When you are different, it can be tough. You may feel as though you are not fitting in with other people as easily or seamlessly as you wish—or that you do not fit in at all. Being left out or excluded, feeling judged or regarded as "other"—all of these experiences can make you feel unwelcome. Sometimes this can lead you to overfocus on your difference and ignore the other parts of yourself. That is why it is so important to remember that your difference is not your entire self—it is just one of many parts of you. If your difference causes you challenges, please know that you are not alone. Many of us have differences; some are visible and others are not. Whatever your difference might be, you are a good and valuable person in all your many facets—and you have a difference—just like everyone else!

## MY DIFFERENCE IS NOT ALL OF ME

This activity will help you to connect with the truth of who you are and practice honoring all parts of you.

- Get comfortable in the space and place you are in right now.

- Slowly breathe in for 3 counts and breathe out for 5 counts for one minute.

- If it would feel good to you, stretch or move your body for a few moments. Just give your body what it may need right now.

- Now, write a self-compassionate letter to yourself about your difference. Describe how it makes you feel different.

- Now list some things about your difference that are positive or that you have learned from.

- How might your difference help you connect with others instead of feeling separate?

## REFLECTION ZONE

- Jot down what you observed and noticed about yourself during today's activity.................................................................................................

- What thoughts came up for you during this activity?..............................

.................................................................................................................

- How did your body feel during this activity? (For examples, you can refer to the list on page 13.) ........................................................................

.................................................................................................................

- What feelings and emotions did you notice during this activity? (For examples, you can refer to the lists on pages 12–13.)

.................................................................................................................

- What did you learn about yourself that really stood out to you?

.................................................................................................................

- Did you find any parts of today's activity that you would like to keep as go-tos when feeling different hurts? If so, jot down your keepers here:

.................................................................................................................

- Jot down your word to carry with you to remind you that you are not your difference. ...........................................................................................

## CHECKING IN WITH MYSELF AFTER EXPLORING TODAY'S ACTIVITY

**Circle the number below that describes how you are feeling right now.**

| 5=feeling really good now | 4=feeling good now | 3=feeling ok now | 2=not feeling good now | 1=really struggling now |

You explored this activity
and yourself—so cool!

# A SOFT LANDING AFTER A HARD DAY

## CHECKING IN WITH MYSELF BEFORE EXPLORING TODAY'S ACTIVITY

**Circle the number below that describes how you are feeling right now.**

5=feeling really good now          4=feeling good now          3=feeling ok now          2=not feeling good now          1=really struggling now

Everyone has totally crappy days from time to time. Sometimes several days in a row! Whatever you are feeling during these times will not last forever, even though it may seem like it will never end. When you're feeling beaten up, worn out, overwhelmed, or like you need a break, it can be tempting to be "tough" and just keep on going—but that's when your body and mind really need some love. Self-compassion is about responding to your hard days with self-kindness. When life is hard, counter with its opposite—some softness. Instead of playing the "I'm so tough" card or punishing yourself even more, how about responding to yourself kindly, as a good friend would, with a soft landing?

Having some soft landing ideas at hand means you are ready to respond softly when you have had a hard experience. Perhaps visiting a soothing space, doing something creative, sitting with a cup of herbal tea, reading a favorite book, listening to music that uplifts you, or another activity that makes you feel good. This time spent doing something positive with yourself can totally help you recharge, reconnect with your truest self, and find some peace.

## MY SOFT LANDING

This activity is about connecting to softness when you have had a hard day.

- Get comfortable in the space and place you are in right now.
- Slowly breathe in for 3 counts and breathe out for 5 counts for one minute.
- If it would feel good to you, stretch or move your body for a few moments. Just give your body what it may need right now.
- Now, sketch or write down 2 or 3 ways you could respond to yourself with softness when you have hard days.

# REFLECTION ZONE

- Jot down what you observed and noticed about yourself during today's activity. ....................................................................................................

- What thoughts came up for you during this activity? ...............................

  ....................................................................................................

- How did your body feel during this activity? (For examples, you can refer to the list on page 13.) ........................................................................

  ....................................................................................................

- What feelings and emotions did you notice during this activity? (For examples, you can refer to the lists on pages 12–13.)

  ....................................................................................................

- What did you learn about yourself that really stood out to you?

  ....................................................................................................

- Did you find any parts of today's activity that you would like to keep as go-tos when you need a soft landing? If so, jot down your keepers here:

  ....................................................................................................

- Jot down your soft landing word to carry with you for whenever you need it. ...........................................................................................

## CHECKING IN WITH MYSELF AFTER EXPLORING TODAY'S ACTIVITY

**Circle the number below that describes how you are feeling right now.**

| 5=feeling really good now | 4=feeling good now | 3=feeling ok now | 2=not feeling good now | 1=really struggling now |

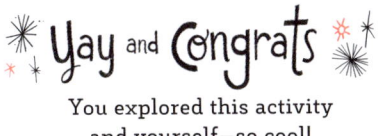

You explored this activity
and yourself—so cool!

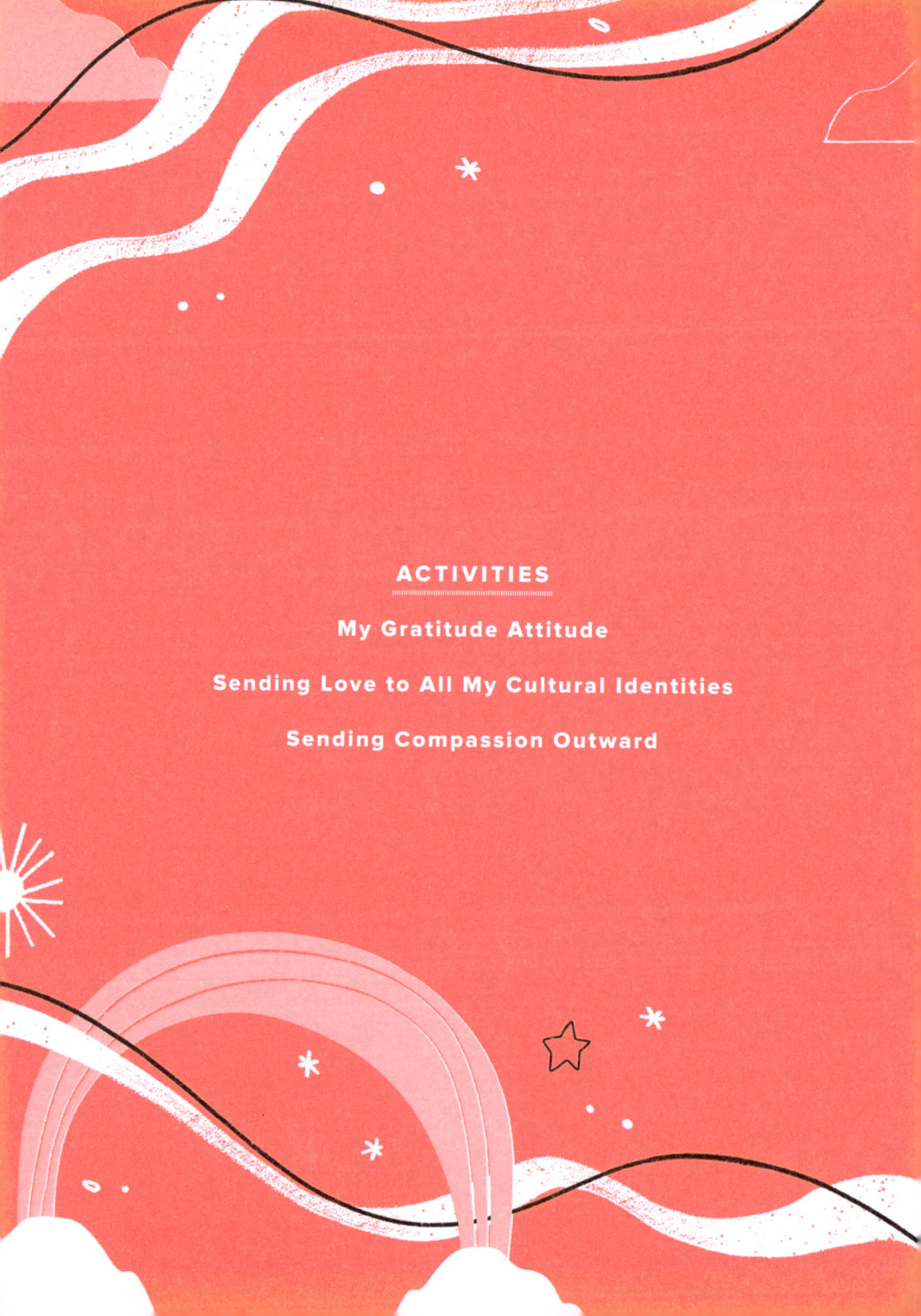

**ACTIVITIES**

My Gratitude Attitude

Sending Love to All My Cultural Identities

Sending Compassion Outward

# ADVENTURE #8:
## Living the Dream of Me with Self-Compassion

# MY GRATITUDE ATTITUDE

Feeling grateful is a powerful way to be self-compassionate. When you turn up the volume on noticing and feeling the things that you are truly thankful for day-to-day, it can totally reframe your outlook and make you feel good. It is so easy to overfocus on negative things, but doing so has a negative effect on your mood. Instead, try to remember all the things, large and small, you may have gratitude for in your life. This will help you to have a gratitude attitude, which is a very effective way of shifting your mind, body, and emotions out of the weeds and into the beauty of being in balance.

## WHAT I'M GRATEFUL FOR

This activity is an opportunity to reflect upon and explore the things you are grateful for so you can amp up your gratitude attitude.

- Get comfortable in the space and place you are in right now.
- Slowly breathe in for 3 counts and breathe out for 5 counts for one minute.
- If it would feel good to you, stretch or move your body for a few moments. Just give your body what it may need right now.
- Press your stop-and-notice button and mindfully reflect on at least 3 small things and 3 big things you have gratitude for in your world. These are things that you would deeply miss if they were not there.
- Write down these 6 gratitude points and what it is about each one that you feel thankful about.
- Read over your gratitude points and reflect on how they can help you maintain a gratitude attitude.

# REFLECTION ZONE

- Jot down what you observed and noticed about yourself during today's activity...................................................................................................

- What thoughts came up for you during this activity?..............................
...............................................................................................................

- How did your body feel during this activity? (For examples, you can refer to the list on page 13.) .........................................................................
...............................................................................................................

- What feelings and emotions did you notice during this activity? (For examples, you can refer to the lists on pages 12–13.)
...............................................................................................................

- What did you learn about yourself that really stood out to you?
...............................................................................................................

- Did you find any parts of today's activity that you would like to keep as go-tos when remembering that your gratitude attitude would be helpful thing? If so, jot down your keepers here: .................................................
...............................................................................................................

- Jot down your favorite gratitude attitude word to carry with you.
...............................................................................................................

## CHECKING IN WITH MYSELF AFTER EXPLORING TODAY'S ACTIVITY

**Circle the number below that describes how you are feeling right now.**

| 5=feeling really good now | 4=feeling good now | 3=feeling ok now | 2=not feeling good now | 1=really struggling now |

Yay and Congrats

You explored this activity
and yourself—so cool!

# SENDING LOVE TO ALL MY CULTURAL IDENTITIES

As you know, you have multiple social and cultural identities including gender, race, social class, age, sexual orientation, ability, nationality, immigration status, personality, and others. These identities all interact with one another and the various parts of you. For example, your gender identity has shaped how you experience the world and how other people may view or treat you. The same is true for all of your identities. However, if you look at each of them, you may find that you are more comfortable with some of your identities than others. The identities that you may have some discomfort around are also shaping your experience. It is important to learn to be kind to all of your cultural-social identities since they are all in the mix of what makes you who you are inside and outside. And the uniqueness of you is your superpower!

## LOVING ALL THE PARTS OF ME

Today's activity is an invitation for you to reflect upon all of your cultural-social identities and send them some love.

- Get comfortable in the space and place you are in right now.
- Slowly breathe in for 3 counts and breathe out for 5 counts for one minute.
- If it would feel good to you, stretch or move your body for a few moments. Just give your body what it may need right now.
- Reflect upon the cultural-social identities that you own.
- Now, begin to list every one of your identities.

- Next to each identity, write down a few phrases of appreciation, love, and kindness—even, and especially, if it is challenging to do so.
- Review your list and feel the love.

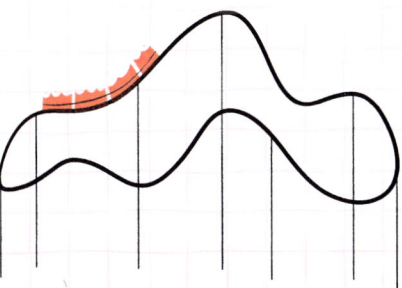

# REFLECTION ZONE

- Jot down what you observed and noticed about yourself during today's activity. ........................................................................................................

- What thoughts came up for you during this activity? ..............................

  ........................................................................................................

- How did your body feel during this activity? (For examples, you can refer to the list on page 13.) ....................................................................

  ........................................................................................................

- What feelings and emotions did you notice during this activity? (For examples, you can refer to the lists on pages 12–13.)

  ........................................................................................................

- What did you learn about yourself that really stood out to you?

  ........................................................................................................

- Did you find any parts of today's activity that you would like to keep as go-tos when feeling your cultural identities? If so, jot down your keepers here: ..............................................................................................

  ........................................................................................................

- Jot down a word or phrase of love for your cultural identities.

  ........................................................................................................

## CHECKING IN WITH MYSELF AFTER EXPLORING TODAY'S ACTIVITY

**Circle the number below that describes how you are feeling right now.**

| 5=feeling really good now | 4=feeling good now | 3=feeling ok now | 2=not feeling good now | 1=really struggling now |

**Yay and Congrats**

You explored this activity and yourself—so cool!

# SENDING COMPASSION OUTWARD

Now that you have completed your personal self-compassion journal adventures, you are invited to also extend that sense of compassion to others in your orbit—your family, your friends, all of the beings you encounter in your life! Every single human being struggles at times. Some of them have experienced and may currently be facing far greater challenges than others. Struggling is a natural part of living, no matter what age you are or what situation you are in. And all humans need and seek out kindness, love, and compassion—this is the true nature of connection—and connecting is an essential part of living. And you will likely find that being able to show some compassion to others in your life will reflect back on you in positive ways.

## SPREADING THE LOVE

This final activity is an invitation for you to spread some of the compassion you have developed to others—your family, friends, and beyond.

- Get comfortable in the space and place you are in right now.
- Slowly breathe in for 3 counts and breathe out for 5 counts for one minute.
- If it would feel good to you, stretch or move your body for a few moments. Just give your body what it may need right now.
- Choose at least two people in your orbit who may need some compassion right now.
- Jot down the names of these two people and what you think they might need.

- Write down how you will show your gifts of compassion, love, and kindness toward them.

- Set a time to bring the compassion. When you've done it, write down how it made you feel.

# REFLECTION ZONE

- Jot down what you observed and noticed about yourself during today's activity. ........................................................................................................

- What thoughts came up for you during this activity? ..............................
  ........................................................................................................

- How did your body feel during this activity? (For examples, you can refer to the list on page 13.) ..................................................................
  ........................................................................................................

- What feelings and emotions did you notice during this activity? (For examples, you can refer to the lists on pages 12–13.)
  ........................................................................................................

- What did you learn about yourself that really stood out to you?
  ........................................................................................................

- Did you find any parts of today's activity that you would like to keep as go-tos when sending compassion toward others? If so, jot down your keepers here: ...............................................................................................
  ........................................................................................................

- Jot down a word of kindness that you will carry with you to remind you to show compassion toward others. .............................................................

## CHECKING IN WITH MYSELF AFTER EXPLORING TODAY'S ACTIVITY

**Circle the number below that describes how you are feeling right now.**

| 5=feeling really good now | 4=feeling good now | 3=feeling ok now | 2=not feeling good now | 1=really struggling now |

**Yay** and **Congrats**
You explored this activity
and yourself—so cool!

# MY KEEPERS

A big congratulations to you on taking this adventure! Now that you have worked your way through this journal, here is a place for you to write down your keepers, the most memorable things you learned from your self-compassion journey.

Before you begin, I have a keeper to share. My keeper for you is to always remember that you are golden—valuable, worthy, and precious. It does not matter what you look like or what you have accomplished or anything else. The more you learn to be comfortable with who you are over time, the more your own golden self will begin to really shine. Then you will be able to illuminate your true light into the world.

Use this space to sketch or jot down anything you learned that you want to remember and take with you. On the next page, try to list 12 keepers that will help you to treat yourself with understanding, kindness, and compassion.

List your top 12 self-compassion keepers for future use:

1. _____

2. _____

3. _____

4. _____

5. _____

6. _____

7. _____

8. _____

9. _____

10. _____

11. _____

12. _____

# RESOURCES AND REFERENCES

## FEELINGS, EMOTIONS, AND BODILY SENSATIONS LISTS

Hoffman Institute Feelings List and Body Sensations:
hoffmaninstitute.org/wp-content/uploads
/Practices-FeelingsSensations.pdf

Wikipedia List of Emotions:
simple.wikipedia.org/wiki/List_of_emotions

Six Seconds—Plutchik's Wheel of Emotions:
6seconds.org/2020/08/11/plutchik-wheel-emotions

## SAFETY AND BRAVERY RESOURCES FOR WHEN YOU NEED HELP

List of Suicide or Crisis Hotlines Around the World:
en.wikipedia.org/wiki/List_of_suicide_crisis_lines

National Suicide Hotline (United States): 1-800-784-2433
National Suicide Prevention Lifeline: 1-800-273-8255
Both are toll-free, 24-hour, confidential hotlines that connect you to a trained counselor at the nearest suicide crisis center. You can also call, text, or chat 988.

The Canada Suicide Prevention Service: 1-833-456-4566
Text: 45645
Phone line available 24 hours. Texting available 4 p.m. to midnight ET.

BetterHelp Online Therapy: betterhelp.com

Depression and Bipolar Support Alliance for Young Adults: dbsalliance.org/support/young-adults

Here to Help (teens and young adults in Canada): heretohelp.bc.ca/infosheet/for-young-adults
-dealing-with-anxiety

The Jed Foundation for Teens and Young Adults:
jedfoundation.org

Society for Adolescent Health and Medicine: Mental Health Resources for Adolescents and Young Adults:
www.adolescenthealth.org/Resources/Clinical-Care
-Resources/Mental-Health/Mental-Health-Resources
-For-Adolesc.aspx

Substance Abuse and Mental Health Services Administration (SAMHA) National Helpline
(United States): 1-800-662-4357
samhsa.gov/find-help/national-helpline

Talkspace Online Therapy: talkspace.com/online-therapy

Teen Counseling: teencounseling.com

## CULTURAL AND SOCIAL IDENTITY RESOURCES

Online Counseling Programs—Mental Health Resources for Young People of Color: onlinecounselingprograms.com
/resources/mental-health-resources-students-of-color

Mental Health America—Asian American/Pacific Islander Communities and Mental Health: mhanational.org/issues
/asian-americanpacific-islander-communities-and
-mental-health

Black Mental Health Alliance: blackmentalhealth.com

Therapy for Black Girls: therapyforblackgirls.com

National Alliance on Mental Health—Hispanic/Latinx:
nami.org/Your-Journey/Identity-and-Cultural-Dimensions
/Hispanic-Latinx

Latinx Therapy: latinxtherapy.com

We R Native: wernative.org

Centers for Disease Control and Prevention—National Center for Health Statistics: cdc.gov/nchs/nhis
/sexual_orientation/background.htm

National Center for Transgender Equality:
transequality.org

The Trevor Project (LGBTQIA2S+): thetrevorproject.org

Dreamscape Foundation—Adjusting to Challenges of Being a Young Adult with Disabilities:
dreamscapefoundation.org/adjusting-to-challenges
-of-being-a-young-adult-with-disabilities

Easterseals Services for Young Adults with Disabilities:
easterseals.com/our-programs/adult-services
/services-for-younger-adults.html

Neurodiversity Hub: neurodiversityhub.org

JDRF—Support for Teens with Type 1 Diabetes:
jdrf.org/t1d-resources/newly-diagnosed/teens

## MINDFULNESS APPS

Breethe
Calm
Headspace
iBreathe
INSCAPE
Liberate
Stop Breathe Think

## SELF-COMPASSION BOOKS

Bluth, K. (2020). *The Self-Compassionate Teen: Mindfulness and Compassion Skills to Conquer Your Critical Inner Voice.* Oakland, CA: New Harbinger Publications.

Bluth, K., & Neff, K. (2017). *Self-Compassion Workbook for Teens: Mindfulness and Compassion Skills to Overcome Self-Criticism and Embrace Who You Are.* Oakland, CA: New Harbinger Publications.

Germer, C. (2009). *The Mindful Path to Self-Compassion: Freeing Yourself from Destructive Thoughts and Emotions.* New York, NY: The Guilford Press.

Hickman, S. (2021). *Self-Compassion for Dummies.* Hoboken, NJ: John Wiley and Sons.

Neff, K. (2021). *Fierce Self-Compassion: How Women Can Harness Kindness to Speak Up, Claim Their Power, and Thrive.* New York, NY: Harper.

Neff, K. (2015). *Self-Compassion: The Proven Power of Being Kind to Yourself.* New York, NY: William Morrow.

Neff, K., & Germer, C. (2018). *The Mindful Self-Compassion Workbook: A Proven Way to Accept Yourself, Build Inner Strength, and Thrive.* New York, NY: The Guilford Press.

# ACKNOWLEDGMENTS

I wholeheartedly acknowledge the developers of Mindful Self-Compassion (MSC), Dr. Kristin Neff and Dr. Christopher Germer. Without their brilliant vision for cultivating greater self-compassion in the world, this book would not exist. I also want to extend deep gratitude for all the wisdom they have shared through their self-compassion teachings with undying dedication to supporting diversity, equity, inclusion, and belonging. Additionally, I am deeply appreciative of my supervisor, Dr. Steven Hickman, Executive Director at the Center for Mindful Self-Compassion. He has been a wonderful mentor who has truly advanced my MSC teaching abilities and provided opportunities that greatly expanded my organizational and personal diversity and equity work. I owe much gratitude to my dear colleague and diversity co-teacher, Dr. Tracy Ochester, Coordinator and Developer of Midwest Alliance for Mindfulness. Dr. Ochester has always expressed a deep sense of heart and soul as a human being in addition to modeling a true example of a wise and compassionate mindfulness teacher. I want to send deep gratitude to all my students and colleagues at the University of Kansas—School of Social Welfare. My work at this institution over the last seventeen years has been an enormous part of the inspiration for this book.

A very sincere thanks to Sharyn Rosart, Rachelle Longé McGhee, Alison Keefe, and Alicia Terry at Spruce Books.

Finally, I have enormous gratitude for the love and support of my precious family members and ancestors, and the deep, underlying root system that has sustained their will to survive and thrive. As a cisgender Black-multiracial woman, this has truly supported my ability to mindfully acknowledge the times of pain and learn from discomfort with self-compassion. I want to thank, acknowledge, and celebrate my entire family for their determination and resilience, especially Mom, Daddy, Susan, Chester, Christy, Kelly, Elise, Elizabeth, Jesse, Mama Sil, Edward, and Papa Dimp.

# AFTERWORD

When I was a little girl, I absolutely loved to line up all my stuffed animals and dolls on my bed and pretend I was their teacher because I was so intrigued by my elementary school teachers. I loved the way teachers helped students gain more awareness about themselves and the world in so many ways. Teaching was a way to inspire and expand young hearts and minds to the diverse realities of different communities, cultures, places, and spaces. I became an elementary teacher and worked with second and fifth graders. The core of my work was not only to teach my class math, science, and reading, but also the foundational lesson that they were good kids with many talents. I remember inviting all the kids in my classroom to repeat over and over the phrase "Yes, I can," even when some of them did not believe it. I also worked to inspire the kids who had a history of always getting into trouble and acting out at school. I spent as much time as I could supporting them because I knew what it felt like to be negatively dismissed and minimized as a Black female. My deepest pain was informing my deepest need, their deepest need, and my call to human service. I knew these kids needed to experience a different story about themselves.

Fast-forward to the present and I can now declare that I have always been true to teaching, presenting, human service, social justice, and learning how to live out my own story of truth. I am an avid practitioner of mindfulness, yoga, social justice advocacy, and self-compassion. I am so glad that I discovered the powerful practice of self-compassion, especially during a time when I had experienced many family losses. I learned over time that self-compassion was a very useful resource that informed what I really needed in the moment to self-soothe and/or take wise action. As a result I have worked to bring greater well-being to many social work students, psychotherapy clients, underserved communities, war veterans, survivors of traumas, yoga students, diversity initiatives, organizations, businesses, agencies, and mindfulness participants of all ages.

tention in writing this book is to extend compassionate support for those e need and courage to create and authentically live their stories of truth, edom.